Inner Child Healing Companion Workbook

Practical Self-Therapy Exercises For
Daughters Of Narcissistic Mothers

Ella Lansville

This book is intended for personal use only. The goal of this book is to help create a community of survivors who can share their journeys and reach other people with similar stories. Please note that, while the author is speaking from personal experience and extensive research, this book is not a substitute for professional mental health care.

If your mental health has made you worried about your safety, please contact emergency health services immediately.

Disclaimer Notice:

Everything included in this book is factual and up to date as far as the author and publisher are aware. By reading this, you acknowledge that the author is not speaking from the position of a trained mental health expert, nor is the author giving any medical advice. If you are hesitant to attempt any of the methods found in this book, reach out to a mental health professional before going forward.

By reading this book, you are agreeing to take responsibility for any possible damages that may occur as a result of the information presented. The author is not responsible in any way for direct or indirect damages, including any misinformation or omissions that may be found.

The names in this book have been changed out of respect for the privacy of the individuals involved.

Contents

Introduction   1

1. Discovering Your Inner Child   12

2. Life As A Scapegoat   28

3. Mindful Practices to Heal Emotional Neglect   43
    Wounds

4. Identifying the Signs of Your Wounded Inner Child   58

5. Uncovering Your Authentic Self   73

6. Going Through the Stages   91

7. Reshaping Your Childhood   120

8. Breaking Unhealthy Childhood Patterns   132

9. Working Through Your Triggers   154

10. Internal Family Systems Exercises   170

11. How You Can Re-parent Your Inner Child   186

Epilogue   202

About Author   205

References

Introduction

As I look into my mind, I see a girl, no more than eighteen, standing in front of me. She does not see me, but I am overwhelmed by the number of emotions that flood through me at that moment. The girl closes the front door behind her, a gray backpack swung over one shoulder while the other shoulder slouches. Her head is down, and she looks pointedly at the floor, ignoring the gaze of anyone who could be approaching.

As she continues walking through the hallways of her childhood home, she keeps her eyes trained on the ground. Every step brings her closer to her bedroom door and peace and quiet. But within a few seconds, the girl hears footsteps approaching her. She stops in her tracks, merely a few feet from her bedroom, but she cannot escape unnoticed now. Reluctantly, but with what she hopes is a stern, tough face, she raises her head and meets her mother's eyes.

The girl has become used to conversations like these throughout her life, especially coming from her mother. She can recall the various times that her mother has belittled her, lied to her, and used her, but she is at a point where she is used to the attacks. Her one goal at this point is to leave. She does not know where yet, or if it is possible, but she goes through every day with the hope of something greater at the forefront of her mind. When things become overwhelming, the girl remembers her goal and convinces herself that it is not just a possibility but an inevitability.

Her mother's face is filled with an emotion that the girl cannot identify at first. Her gaze is powerful, burning into the girl's eyes as though she had been looking at the sun for too long. Despite this, she meets her mother's gaze and tries to appear neutral. There is something she needs to say but cannot bring herself to, fearing her mother's reaction. No matter how hard she tries, she knows that her mother will see right through her, somehow knowing that something was wrong even when her daughter did her best to hide this.

The mother remains with a mask on her face. Though she might appear calm to another, the daughter knows her well enough, knows that even her kindest smile could be hiding malice. Still, the girl holds out hope as her mother's expression transforms into that of worry. Her eyes widen, her lips turn slightly downwards, her heavy breaths akin to sighs of relief, of joy, of gratefulness.

"I was so worried about you," her mother tells her, and the concern in her voice is real, or it seems that way. Her words are grim, her tone genuine, her words laced with fear. Despite this, the girl hesitates. She is not afraid of this side of her mother, but rather the knowledge that her mother's mood may shift in an instant if she says the wrong thing. "Why did you turn off your phone? I must have called you nearly a hundred times and left almost as many messages. Do you know how afraid I was that something had happened?"

The girl had expected as much as soon as she had made the decision to switch her device off earlier but chose to proceed anyway. She had news, news that she did not want to divulge to her mother but that she knew she would have to regardless. Though her mother still wears a mask of concern, the girl can pick up on little giveaways hidden underneath, the signs of irritation and disappointment beginning to show through. There is no escaping this situation now, no matter what she does or says.

The girl's mother gives her one more quizzical glance before speaking once again. "What is it?" Her voice has shifted now, ever so slightly different from her previously concerned tone. The concern is there, but the kindness in her voice seems forced, and the girl notices something more sinister hidden behind it.

After a few tense beats, the girl inhales and considers her words. She opens her mouth, but the words fly away from her mind, and she cannot bring herself to speak until she hears her mother's voice again: "Tell me."

The girl nods, clearing her throat. "I didn't get accepted," she says in a rush, hoping her mother will mistake her words for something else. Discussions of studying at a university have begun recently, and life has become a nightmare for the girl. This is her chance, her opportunity, to leave and not return. In her head, she dreams of a life where she wakes up and, for once, has no other worries in the world.

Her mother is vehemently against this. She wants her daughter to stay close, to stay in this house, this house that makes it hard for her to breathe some days. Her mother insists that she goes to the local community college, the one that is only a short ride away, the one where the girl will know everyone and everyone will know her, the place where she would leave and come home only to suffer more. She would do anything to avoid that fate.

Her mother scoffs, and the girl knows the words that will come next. "See? All of that studying for nothing. I told you that you were wasting your time. But you think your mother is your enemy, don't you? You won't take my advice, even when you know I'm right." She lets out a sigh, frustrated this time, no longer holding back her thinly veiled irritation.

The girl waits for what comes next, knowing that her mother is not finished just yet. Her mother squeezes her eyes shut, taking a deep breath like her daughter is exhausting her. "I only want the best for you," she says, and for a moment, the girl wants more than anything to believe these words. "When will you finally understand?"

Her mother scoffs, and the irritation behind it feels almost suffocating to the girl. "You're stubborn just like your father," she spits out, intending to wound her daughter. "Of course, you inherited his character. You even look just like him."

The girl prays that the conversation will end now, but knows she will not be so lucky. Her mother sighs, getting caught up in the throes of her dramatics. That was one of her mother's key characteristics: the ability to make a slight error seem like the worst, most heinous offense in history.

"You can't do any better than community college, you know that? You're wasting your time. All the money I put into your education, only for you to give me no appreciation or effort in return. You have all the chances I never had at your age, and you're still ungrateful for all the sacrifices I've made to raise you. You really are just like *him*." There is a brief silence, indicating that the girl's mother is finished with her rant. The girl took a deep breath that she had been holding during her mother's momentary speech.

"I'm sorry," the girl says because she never knows what else to say. She learned long ago that no matter what she said, nothing could make her mother's mood change. Usually, she sticks to an apologetic "I'm sorry" to avoid further conflict, accepting her mother's words until her mother has finally given up on the discussion. Her mother simply sighs in response, and the two fall into silence for a few solemn moments.

"Don't disappoint me," her mother says, breaking the silence between them. The daughter nods, unable to think of any other words to tell her. Her mother walks away from her, and the girl finally escapes to her bedroom, the only place where she feels a semblance of calm. With every step she takes to her door, the girl tells herself one thing: *Get out. Leave, run, never come back.*

After a moment, she accepts this wound. She adds it to the long list of the ones she has collected throughout her life, then buries the list as far into the recesses of her mind as she can reach. She knows that one day, this list will present itself to her, and she will have to face the feelings she has run from for so long. But today is not that day, and she carries on to her room, her mind blank.

· · · ● · ● · · · ·

When I think of children like that girl, I see myself reflected in them. I toss this memory around inside my head, pondering other moments in time when that girl was hurt by her mother. There are plenty of times that I have forgotten and plenty of instances where I am certain the girl can remember a wound to which I have long since lost access. Regardless, when I look into the girl's eyes, I feel like I know her. For a long time, this feeling was not merely uncomfortable, but terrifying. I spent years running from this feeling, from the sense that I knew this child, that she still lived inside of me.

As I continued to grow into adulthood and educate myself on maternal narcissistic abuse, many unpleasant emotions began to arise. The more I remembered things, the angrier I was–at my mother, at myself, and at the inner child within me who refused to let the past go. It got to the point where I felt despondent, as if all the hope had been sucked out of me. I could not ignore my mother's impact on my psyche and self-worth anymore. Because of this, I found myself unintentionally lashing out at my inner child in an attempt to deny the truth, blaming her for things outside of our control, and acting out to prove something to her, and myself, about how I was no longer the same person.

The previous book of this two-part series on the inner child primarily discussed growing up as the scapegoat daughter of a narcissistic mother and the inner child wounds you sustained be-cause of that experience. Through the compassionate guide, you have learned essential information about the types of inner child wounds, the scapegoat child in a narcissistic family unit, and how childhood neglect impacts the person you become as an adult.

Additionally, the guide offered insights into why it is so vital to reconnect with your wounded inner child. As the daughter of a narcissistic mother, your inner child has held on to all the wounds you have buried. As a result of the neglect you faced as a child, you adapted harmful coping mechanisms to use when triggered. You constantly push away the emotions associated with your inner child's memories and force your inner child to hide in the back of your mind and never speak up. While willfully ignoring your inner child provides you with temporary relief, your emotions will undoubtedly return tenfold.

Though you are aware of the essence of reconnecting with your inner child and the reasons why you must do so to complete your healing journey, your final step towards healing will require practice. Simply learning about the psychology of the inner child is informative, but without exercises to actively implement inner child work techniques into your life, you may be hesitant to take action.

Therefore, this book will act as a companion to the previous book and go through the topics presented in the guide to offer specialized exercises and interactive material to heal your inner child.

The exercises and practices present in this workbook aim to help scapegoat daughters of narcissistic mothers. As a scapegoat daughter myself, I have found value in many of these exercises for communicating with my inner child. The wounds sustained as a scapegoat in a narcissistic family system are severe, and a nuanced, customized approach to healing your scapegoat inner child is necessary. That is what I hope to offer with the suggestions throughout this workbook.

As you work through the exercises in this book, there are a few things that you should remind yourself about. Given the challenging nature of inner child work and the overwhelming emotions it may cause, you need to understand how to work with the book in the most comfortable way.

I recommend that you go through these exercises slowly and carefully. Ensure that you understand an exercise and its purpose before you engage. If you feel uncomfortable at any point during an exercise, take a deep breath, mark the page, walk away from the book, and take a well-deserved break. Return to the exercise when you feel rested and ready to continue.

Furthermore, this workbook will be more effective if you practice self-care techniques every single day. As opposed to the previous workbook in this series named *Self-Care Workbook For Daughters Of Narcissistic Mothers*, this workbook will discuss self-care practices specifically for healing one's inner child. Always prioritize your health and remember that reconnecting with your inner child will take time. This workbook will help you build trust with your inner child and learn to care for your child and adult self simultaneously.

If you have followed this series up until this point, or if you find value within this workbook specifically, I encourage you to leave a review on Amazon, if possible. The feedback offered in the reviews is essential to my work and to constantly improving myself and understanding my experiences and the experiences of the community of daughters around me. By offering new perspectives and experiences with maternal narcissistic abuse, you can help create a well-rounded and thorough view of daughters of narcissistic mothers and the inner child.

Additionally, your review will help other daughters of narcissistic mothers know they are not alone. There are other survivors out there–probably more than you may think. Showing support for this book allows me to continue growing a community of warriors that have bravely stood against narcissistic abuse.

Always remember that you are brave and resilient for allowing yourself to heal from maternal narcissistic abuse. Your unwavering strength in the face of obstacles proves your ability to overcome anything thrown your way. With time and patience, you can heal and reconcile with your wounded inner child. Even if it takes time, the reconciliation between you and your inner child is inevitable.

By accepting this, you are committing yourself to newfound happiness and loving your inner child and yourself. I wish you all the best as you embark on this step on the pathway to ultimate healing.

Chapter One

Discovering Your Inner Child

T O BEGIN INNER CHILD work, you must start with the basics before moving on to more advanced exercises. Initial contact with your inner child is crucial to moving forward in your healing journey. You are on the right path, even if you can only discover a small part of your inner child with the exercises in this chapter. Before getting into the exercises, I have provided a brief recap of the sections from the *Inner Child Healing Guide* that correlate with the exercises in this chapter.

Brief Overview of Topics

The exercises contained in this chapter cover a few specific topics that correlate with the topics in the *Inner Child Healing Guide*.

Begin by recalling the initial definition of the inner child. Scapegoat daughters of narcissistic mothers carry inner child wounds. Though the inner child exists within everybody, daughters of narcissistic mothers carry the weight of years' worth of childhood wounds. The idea of the inner child's existence originated from psychologist Carl Jung and is thought of by many as the part of one's psyche that has not yet grown up, potentially because of the impact of childhood abuse.

While you may not have consciously initiated contact with your wounded inner child, she is undoubtedly suffering due to your mother's abuse and your cycle of denial, where you cannot face and accept your inner child's painful emotions. In the *Inner Child Healing Guide*, you learned about the four primary types of inner child wounds: abandonment, guilt, trust, and neglect wounds. Exercises for inner child healing may differ based on addressing a specific type of child wound, but ultimately, these wounds hold you back from having a healthy inner child.

Regularly practicing inner child healing work will help you understand what constitutes a healthy inner child. Though the exercises in this workbook will delve deeper into the idea of improving your inner child's health, the core attribute of a healthy inner child is her happiness and willingness to explore opportunities. Remember that there is hope for you and your inner child to reconcile and heal, hand in hand. Individually, you are both strong and resilient, but together, you are an unstoppable force.

Exercises For Identifying Types of Inner Child Wounds

To begin, it is helpful to complete a set of brief exercises to identify the types of inner child wounds you suffer from. By identifying your inner child wounds concretely and comprehensively, you can start noticing how inner child wounds manifest in your adult life. I have found that listing out the types of inner child wounds and connecting some of my childhood experiences with a particular type of wound helps me get to the root of my issue.

For instance, if you were to recall a scenario where your mother blamed you for her relationship falling apart, you would likely place the wound into the guilt category. This helps you not only understand the event that wounded you, but the core emotion behind *why* it wounded you.

Exercise to Identify Abandonment Wounds

Below is an exercise where you can start identifying your inner child's abandonment wounds. To begin with, list some words or thoughts that come to mind when you think of abandonment. For instance, one might associate abandonment with loneliness, sadness, fear, or confusion. After that, you can start incorporating details about childhood memories and how they relate to the selected words. If you are struggling to recall specific instances or feel that some instances are too overwhelming to address at this stage, then think of any scenario that would make someone feel abandoned. Finally, try to identify how your abandonment wounds manifest in your adult life, or how remembering abandonment wounds make you feel.

Example

Association Word: *Loneliness*

Childhood Memory: *Thinking of loneliness makes me recall times when my mother communicated that I only had her and that no one else could love me.*

How I Feel As An Adult: *As an adult, I find that I run away from healthy relationships when things get intense because I still fear that my mother was right.*

Now complete this exercise on your own, using a similar template below. Describe three or more associations in as much detail as you can.

Association Word: ✎

Childhood Memory: ✎

How I Feel As An Adult: ✎

Exercise to Identify Guilt Wounds

This section will use the same template, this time focused on feelings of guilt and instances where your narcissistic mother guilted you into feeling or thinking a certain way. Some words and emotions you may choose to associate with guilt include shame, regret, embarrassment, or blameworthy. Again, do not force memories if they do not come naturally to you. The beauty of this exercise is that it is simple enough to return to later in your journey if you uncover new things about your experiences that you want to understand more.

Example

Association Word: *Shame*

Childhood Memory: *The word "shame" reminds me of times when my mother compared me to my "golden child" sibling.*

How I Feel As An Adult: *As an adult, I still feel ashamed when I cannot meet my personal high standards. I compare myself to others in my life, especially coworkers.*

Now complete this exercise on your own, using a similar template below.

Association Word: ✎

Childhood Memory: ✎

How I Feel As An Adult: ✎

Exercise to Identify Trust Wounds

Next, fill out the exercise, focusing specifically on trust wounds you sustained during childhood. One of the biggest challenges I have faced as an adult daughter of a narcissistic mother is relearning how to trust myself and my inner child's hectic emotions. Trusting other people felt impossible. I was supposed to trust my mother above all else, so how could I trust anyone if she had broken her promises?

Trust is key to any relationship, and your relationship with your inner child is no exception. You might associate with positive words when you think of trust. For example, trust can be associated with honesty, love, empathy, certainty, faithfulness, and hopefulness. However, as the daughter of a narcissistic mother, your inner child may have a less positive understanding of trust than others. You may be inclined to associate negative words with trust, such as betrayal, lies, doubt, anxiety, or suspicion. Do not focus too hard on whether the words coming to you are positive or negative. Let yourself feel whatever it is you are feeling.

Example

Association Word: *Lies*

Childhood Memory: *The word "lies" makes me think of times when my mother gaslighted me as a child.*

How I Feel As An Adult: *As an adult, I still struggle to trust others. When I learn to trust someone, I feel hesitant, yet I want to remain hopeful.*

Now complete this exercise on your own, using a similar template below.

Association Word: ✎

Childhood Memory: ✎

How I Feel As An Adult: ✎

Exercise to Identify Neglect Wounds

The final exercise in this section should be used to focus on the wounds you have gained from childhood neglect. Part of your inner child's issue is that she has not been given the tools necessary to take care of her physical and mental health fully. As you have grown into adulthood, you have had to learn the basics of caring for yourself independently.

However, there are many things you did not learn as a child that you might still be unaware of now. To begin determining what your inner child needs to know, you must start by understanding the neglect you went through in childhood.

Some words you might choose to associate with neglect include words like loneliness, lack of care, ignored, unhealthy, invisible, aimless, or confused. Repeated instances of neglect on the part of the mother are at the root of any narcissistic relationship. By opening yourself up to understanding how your mother neglected you, you can determine what you must do to address the needs of your inner child.

Example

Association Word: *Invisible*

Childhood Memory: *The word "invisible" reminds me of how I used to compare my mother to my friends' mothers. While most mothers teach their daughters important life lessons, I was not given the same level of care and attention from my mother.*

How I Feel As An Adult: *As an adult, I often struggle with navigating obstacles in my life and making my own decisions. I don't know who I am at the core and how to take care of my own needs.*

Now complete this exercise on your own using a similar template below.

Association Word: ✎

Childhood Memory: ✎

How I Feel As An Adult: ✎

Exercise For Initial Communication With Your Inner Child

Once you have identified different types of childhood wounds your inner child suffers from, you can slowly immerse yourself into open communication between these two parts of your identity. Initial communication with your inner child will likely not be extensive, and you may not learn much about her. However, this first contact is crucial to introducing yourself and solidifying you as a nurturing and trustworthy figure. Do not push too hard when encouraging your inner child to communicate–she will share more of herself when she is ready. For now, accept what you can get, continue practicing every day, and remind yourself of the massive progress you have made thus far.

In this exercise, I will guide you through basic strategies for initial communication with your inner child by writing a letter to her. During my healing journey and even now, I love to write letters to my inner child. Sometimes they are from my perspective, but other times they are from the perspective of a childhood friend or individual that influenced my childhood significantly. The letter in this exercise will focus on connecting with your inner child through emotional validation.

After a lifetime of having her emotions denied by your mother and unconsciously by your adult self, your inner child has never learned about the importance of emotional validation. To recognize that your inner child can heal, you must begin by giving her the emotional validation that she has not received in her life.

When you validate your inner child, you are communicating the idea to her that you are trustworthy and empathetic and that she can share anything with you without fear of judgment. While the first letter you write will not accomplish all of this, you will find that your inner child's belief in you has grown over time.

Ultimately, this letter should express your desire to know your inner child and to communicate with her. This first letter is all about letting your inner child know that you care for her and wish to connect with her so that you can heal together. Below is an example letter to help inspire you and for you to use as a framework for how you should address your wounded inner child.

Dear Inner Child,

I am sorry it has taken me so long to write to you. I am sorry that you felt you had to suffer alone, without anyone there to nurture or guide you. While I know I should have come to you sooner, I am here to help you now and will not leave your side again. I promise that, through my actions and words, I will prove to you my full dedication to your healing. I am hurting in a way similar to how you are hurting. What we have experienced in our life is unfair and irreversible, but that does not mean our suffering must continue forever.

I fully understand that you might not be in a place where you can trust me yet. No matter your current feelings towards me, I want you to know that your emotions, thoughts, opinions, and everything unique about you are valid and beautiful. Do not feel shame over how you react to the world around you. I accept you as you are, and I do not want you to ever alter your emotions because of me. Feel what you feel and don't hold back. Everything about you is valid. I hope to communicate with you in more depth in the future at whatever pace makes you most comfortable. I hope that with time, you will understand how deeply my care and love for you run. I want to nurture you and take care of you as we heal side-by-side. When you are ready, I cannot wait to begin our journey together.

Sincerely,

Your Adult Self

········

After I wrote my first successful letter to my inner child, I felt a slight change in me. It was nothing major, but my mind and body felt whole somehow like I had discovered a small part of me that I never knew was missing. This letter is what allowed me to make visual contact with my wounded inner child. Though we did not speak to one another in our initial meeting, seeing my inner child was undoubtedly a massive turning point in my journey.

Over time, I found that as I continued writing letters to my inner child, I could sense her from time to time, just barely. I knew she was there but still did not know how I could see her, how to visualize her so that we could speak honestly. As my letter-writing continued, I started incorporating other small techniques into this exercise. After initially writing to my inner child, I would allow myself to close my eyes and look inwards. I breathed deeply, in and out, for as long as I could focus. I intended to see my inner child after connecting with her through my written words.

Your first meeting with your inner child might not happen exactly how you expect it to, as each inner child is equally unique and unpredictable. When I first met my wounded inner child, I was shocked by how much I learned simply by looking at her. I had decided to sit alone in a quiet room that was void of distractions.

Closing my eyes, I began to look inward, focusing hard to see my inner child.

Eventually, a scene came to my head: a young girl, hair down to her waist and her head hanging low in a way that was reminiscent of how I often held myself. Her body was shrinking in on herself as she tried to make herself as small and unnoticeable as she could. Surrounding her was a forest that seemed to extend forever, with tall, ominous trees that blew in the wind. The sky was dark, either from the night or a brewing storm, but the child did not move. She was alone, silent. Without sunlight, I could barely make out her features, yet I knew who she was.

Initially, I was shocked at how still the girl looked. She was no more than ten, but what I could see on her face clued me in because she was carrying more weight than a ten-year-old ever should. Even in the shadows of the night, I noticed how empty her eyes looked–as if her mind was someplace else entirely. She had zoned out completely and did not even know where she was. Still, she did not seem out of place in this environment. In fact, it suited her in a way that surprised me.

Despite my shock, I could rein my hectic thoughts back in and proceed with the exercise. After focusing all of my attention on connecting with my inner child, I began expanding my view so that I could not only see the child and her surroundings but also feel what she felt. Seeing her was not enough–I had to identify the root of her feelings, the core experiences behind the emptiness in her eyes. I focused as hard as possible but still felt nothing as profound or intense as I was hoping for.

Suddenly, a chilly feeling washed over my body. My arms and legs trembled slightly from the sudden change in temperature, but when I touched my skin, it felt normal, even warmer than usual. I realized then that what I felt was the sensation of cold that the girl was feeling. Looking at her again, I realized she was wearing only a light nightgown. Despite the dangers of the forest floor, she was barefoot. I felt a primal instinct at that moment and wanted nothing more than to grab her tight and start warming her so that the cold did not cause her harm. I wanted to take my warmest blanket and wrap it around her shoulders to show her that I was there, that I could take care of her and nurture her.

However, as my mind got caught up in the idea of helping the girl, I felt a shift in her emotions, her mind going into survivor mode as soon as she recognized the feeling of me caring for her. She snapped to attention, like she had been conscious of my presence the entire time, and opened her mouth into a blood-curdling scream. Her fear ripped through her throat as she screamed again and again. She was scared, more scared than I could have predicted.

Here she was, a child, alone in this dark, cold forest with the trees towering above her, taller than she could imagine and without any space to make her escape. She screamed again, letting out her frustration from having to navigate a world that she barely knew, a world that was scary and unpredictable, a world where she would never have a gentle, loving parent by her side.

·····•·•····

My initial contact with my wounded inner child was enlightening and terrifying all at once. However, it showed me that my work had paid off and that if I continued investing in myself and my healing, I could learn to thrive with my inner child at my side. I was on the right path. I was making progress–I was healing. My inner child longed for my care and attention and would be by my side for the journey ahead.

Chapter Two

Life As A Scapegoat

G ROWING UP AS THE scapegoat child in a narcissistic family system is not an easy childhood for anybody. As the scapegoat daughter of a narcissistic mother, you know firsthand how challenging it is to navigate life under the burden of guilt and blame. No matter what happened to your mother, you were always involved. When she messed up, you were to blame. When you messed up, your mistakes were amplified. When your mother doted on your sibling, she refused to share the same energy with you.

In the second chapter of the *Inner Child Healing Guide*, I discussed the scapegoat child in a narcissistic family system and the responsibilities and burdens this child takes. Below is a brief recap of what was discussed in that chapter to go over the purpose of the scapegoat child and what it means to be your mother's scapegoat.

Brief Overview of Topics

Inner child healing, in the context of this workbook, is aimed at healing scapegoat daughters of narcissistic mothers. Among the many roles in a narcissistic family system is the role of a scapegoat child. This child is constantly blamed and shamed for things outside her control while being responsible for the weight of her family's burdens.

A narcissist uses the scapegoat child to deflect their shortcomings and blame the child for the consequences of their actions. The scapegoat child is often parentified and enmeshed with her mother, believing her mother is the only person she can fully trust. In other cases, the scapegoat might be the one who chooses to rebel against her mother, escaping her narcissistic family system and seeing issues where others do not.

The main types of scapegoat children in narcissistic family systems and throughout adulthood fall into the following roles: the caretaker, the problem-solver, the protector, the truth-teller, the perfectionist, the rebel, the collapsed, and the dysregulated warrior.

Among the primary impacts of being a scapegoat child in a narcissistic family system are feelings of toxic shame, trust issues, low self-esteem, relationship issues, and repeated dysfunctional relationship patterns. There is no single reason a narcissistic mother chooses a specific child to be her scapegoat. However, some potential factors behind her selection include resemblance to people the mother dislikes, a child that shows more sensitivity than their siblings, a child that is rebellious and tells the truth, or arbitrary reasons like the child's age, gender, attractiveness, or intelligence.

The Signs of Being the Scapegoat Child

If you know that you grew up with a narcissistic parent but are unsure of your role in the narcissistic family system, go through the following questionnaire and check off any questions that apply to you. Remember that you could have played different roles in your family system throughout childhood. The scapegoat child is commonly chosen because of the narcissist's specific needs at that point in time. Remember also to trust your instinct. This checklist is not meant to be an official consensus on if you were always the scapegoat child, and not all readers will need to use the checklist at all. However, if you find yourself conflicted or doubting your role, consider the following potential signs of being scapegoated.

- Do you blame yourself for everything, including events that you did not have any influence over?
- Do you always feel like others have a bad opinion about you?

- Are you afraid of making decisions because they might result in failure and others will blame you?
- Do you often feel helpless to change anything?
- When you meet someone, do you feel like you cannot trust them even if they show no signs of deceit or any similarities to your mother?
- In your childhood, did you often feel like a walking target for your mother's verbal attacks?
- Have you had relationships with other covert narcissists in your life and only realized after the relationship ended?
- Do you feel like a black sheep or like you are the outsider in any group setting?
- Do you have a pattern of falling for the same type of people? If so, what are some of the characteristics of this 'type'?
- Do you often feel bad about yourself and internally make negative comments about your appearance, personality, or skills?
- Do you feel like you have to help other people before even considering helping yourself?
- Do you take on the role of "parent" in your close relationships, where you feel like you have to nourish the other person but never expect to get the same care in return?
- Did your mother often praise your sibling(s) while also shaming you?
- Can you recall times when your mother gave love to your sibling while neglecting you?
- Are you the only person in your narcissistic family system that seems to recognize your mother's toxic behaviors?

- Do you ignore troubling emotions when they arise or find that you push away any negative thoughts before you get emotional?

Exercise to Identify Negative or Flawed Thinking Patterns

As the daughter of a narcissistic mother, flawed thinking patterns dominated my headspace in my childhood and much of my early adulthood. Constant negative self-talk makes you feel like you have the weight of the world on your shoulders and are crumbling beneath the pressure. The voice in your head says you are not capable enough or good enough for others.

For myself, I got to a stage in my adulthood where my patterns of flawed thinking and negative self-talk became second nature. Unlearning these toxic patterns was only made possible by my connecting with my wounded inner child. This exercise and the exercise in the following section address the flawed thinking patterns and negative self-talk dominating your inner child's psyche.

The below exercise targets flawed thinking patterns and consists of two parts. Do not worry about part two yet–focus your mind on part one only for now, as its completion is necessary to conduct part two.

The following are prompts regarding your relationship with your mother as a child. Each prompt contains a short scenario that you will then react to. Below each prompt is a space for you to fill out your thoughts if you wish to do so. It is best to use your journal for this purpose. Do your best to include as many details as possible, but if you become overwhelmed, take a break and return to the exercise when ready.

Part One

1.   Picture yourself as a child in your mother's home. Imagine that you are playing with your sibling in the living room. You accidentally bump into a small vase that falls off the table, hitting the floor and breaking into a few pieces. It is a minor clean-up, and no one is hurt. However, your mother responds negatively to your mistake and exaggerates its severity. What happens next? What does your mother say to you? How do you respond?

2.   Now, imagine you are an adolescent girl who has just gotten her first period. This is a moment in a girl's life that is as scary as it is exciting, and for many daughters, their closest confidante during this time is their mother. Thinking that your mother will respond positively and help you navigate periods, you go to tell her what happened. However, you do not get the reaction you were hoping for, as your mother begins to make you feel bad for opening up to her. What does she say or do? How do her words or actions make

you feel? What negative thought patterns do you keep with you after leaving this incident?

✎

3.   Next, imagine a scenario in your childhood where you are sitting at the table, waiting for your mother to come home with dinner. She is much later than she said she would be, and you are growing hungrier by the second. Finally, your mother barges through the front door with her purse in hand, but no food in sight for dinner. When she enters the kitchen, you ask her if she got food for dinner like she said she would. Your mother is angry that you asked and were not concerned about her hectic state. What does she say? How do you respond?

✎

4.   Imagine a similar scenario where your mother comes home at night later than expected. She seems visibly upset, and whenever she acts like this, you know you will be the one to listen to her rants. Your mother comes over to you and starts venting about her ex, pouring out details of her life and relationships you have no control over. Once she concludes her story, she waits for you to respond. The issue is that you are not sure what to say that will not make her react badly. What do you say? How do you navigate this situation?

✎

5. Picture your childhood self dressed in fancy clothes. Your mother is by your side, dressed just as fancy, and you enter a banquet hall full of people in expensive gowns and suits. Your mother has told you a few details about this event, but you know you must be on your best behavior. Your mother wants to impress other people with her perfect family, meaning you have no choice but to act exactly how she wants. When she mingles with other adults, you hear your mother say numerous positive, loving things about you and your family. Everything she says seems too good to be true, and she acts completely differently in this environment than she does at home. What does your mother say about you and your family in her conversations? How does that differ from what she would say to you in a private environment?

Part Two

After reflecting on the scenarios in the previous section, take some time to think about any revelations you made about yourself, your inner child, or your mother. Write down some of your mother's words or actions that stood out to you during the exercise. For instance, if you noticed that your mother routinely commented on your appearance, you may write down phrases that she said to you. Additionally, consider some of her broad statements that encouraged you to think a certain way. For example, did your mother tell you that you could not trust anyone else? Did she tell you that no one else besides her could love you? Did she teach you that love is conditional? Could you only earn her affection by doing something for her first?

Ponder your previous answers until you have identified the core of your mother's actions. Essentially, you should determine the hidden messages behind your mother's words to understand the flawed thinking patterns she expressed to you. Once you understand your mother's thinking patterns, continue with this exercise.

Below are more prompts for you to fill out. However, this time, your answers will be formatted differently. All the prompts will focus on identifying how your mother's negative thought patterns correlate with your own and those of your inner child. Understanding how your adult mindset has been influenced by your mother's toxic messages is key to being able to nurture and care for your inner child. When you recognize the negative ideas that you absorbed because of your mother, you can start to move toward developing a healthier, productive mindset.

1. What did your mother say when criticizing your appearance? When you see yourself in a mirror, do you say similar things to yourself? For instance, if you frequently have negative thoughts about your weight, height, hair, or any other part of your physical appearance, can you notice any parallels between your mother's negative talking and your negative self-talk?

✎

2. What did your mother say or do when you made a mistake? For example, if you failed a test in childhood, what would your mother say to exaggerate the situation and shame you? Then, think about a mistake you have made recently, such as an error at work. How did you respond to yourself? Did you tell yourself negative things like "I mess everything up," "I am not smart enough," "I am humiliating myself," or "I am a failure"? Was your response to making a mistake similar to how your mother responded and shamed you in childhood?

✎

3. Imagine that you are a teenager and your mother has recently gone through a painful breakup. What would your mother say to you to make you think the breakup was your fault? How would she blame you for her personal issues? As an adult, think of a time or imagine a scenario when you went through a similarly painful breakup. How do you react to this? What do you say to yourself when a relationship of any kind ends, and how are these words similar to your mother's? For instance, does a breakup prompt you to think things like "Everyone leaves me," "I am unlovable," "My actions alone are to blame for the breakup," "I will be alone forever," etc.?

✎

4. As a child, there were many instances where your mother discouraged you from being honest with yourself and her. Psychological manipulations and gaslighting from a narcissistic mother make

it difficult for you to express yourself freely or develop self-trust. What did your mother say on the occasions when you attempted to open up to her? Did she ignore your problems in a way similar to how you ignore your problems as an adult? Did she shut you down and teach you never to be honest? Has she ever humiliated you after you shared something with her? How did your mother's beliefs about opening up and being vulnerable affect how you interact with people now? Do you find it impossible to open up or develop trust, and what thoughts do you have when you are considering opening yourself up to someone?

5. Recall a time when your mother gaslighted you into thinking that your emotional responses were unwarranted and selfish. For instance, if she said something insensitive, and you shared your discomfort, imagine her telling you that it was only a joke, that you are overreacting and trying to make her feel bad. How do you respond when someone says something that hurts you as an adult? Do you speak up? Do you tell yourself that you are overreacting and making a big deal of nothing?

Exercise to Tackle Negative Self-Talk

While the above exercise for tackling negative thinking patterns and self-talk is essential to understanding the root of your harmful behaviors, sometimes all you need is a quick list to refer to when you find yourself caught up in negative self-talk. Below are some negative phrases you may tell yourself and how you can oppose those phrases with a positive, affirming statement.

Negative Self-Talk: *I hate my body. I wish I could change it.*

Positive Statement: I am in control of my body and beautiful the way I am. I have the power to own my body and treat it with respect.

Negative Self-Talk: *I will never find love.*

Positive Statement: My worth is not based on whether I am deemed to be lovable by other people. I love myself first.

Negative Self-Talk: *I'm overreacting and should not be so upset.*

Positive Statement: My emotions are unquestionably valid, and I cannot let myself or others dictate how I am "allowed" to feel.

Negative Self-Talk: *Everybody hates me.*

Positive Statement: Many people love and care for me, and I love and care for myself.

Negative Self-Talk: *I cannot accomplish my goals, so I should give up trying.*

Positive Statement: I am capable of things beyond my imagination, and I will never know if I am unwilling to try. I work hard to reach my goals and know that things will work out.

Negative Self-Talk: *I am untalented.*

Positive Statement: I have many talents and skills, but my worth is not defined based on these skills.

Negative Self-Talk: *I am not good enough.*

Positive Statement: I am good enough for myself and others. Whatever happens, I do not doubt that I am good enough.

Negative Self-Talk: *I do not deserve happiness.*

Positive Statement: I am as deserving of love and happiness as anyone else. I welcome happiness and love into my life.

Negative Self-Talk: *I am selfish.*

Positive Statement: I should take time to put myself first. I care about the needs of others and help people, but I understand that my mental well-being is most important. Understanding my needs is not selfish.

Negative Self-Talk: *I always mess things up and make mistakes. I am worthless.*

Positive Statement: I am worthy of forgiveness for my mistakes, and I am dedicated to improving myself daily.

· · · · ● · ● · · · ·

To close this chapter, I would like to offer a brief checklist to ensure you monitor your mental state throughout these exercises. You have made incredible progress in this workbook already, but given the heavy nature of this subject, conduct a quick check-in with yourself before moving forward. Before proceeding to the next chapter, review the checklist below to measure your headspace and recenter.

Is my environment still comfortable and soothing?

Does my body feel physically okay?

Am I prepared with food and water if I start feeling depleted?

Is my breathing even?

Am I hydrated?

Am I free of any distractions?

Do I feel okay mentally?

Have I recently had a meal?

Am I well-rested?

Do I feel safe and ready to continue?

Chapter Three

Mindful Practices to Heal Emotional Neglect Wounds

G ROWING UP IN A narcissistic family system means that much of your childhood consisted of emotional neglect from the narcissist. Your mother's emotional neglect wounded your inner child in many ways and gave your inner child a skewed perception of the world, love, and relationships. Emotional neglect may occur when you acted as your mother's parent and were forced into an adult role. Emotional neglect also occurs when your mother does not show you love or guide you throughout childhood. Prolonged emotional neglect has left your inner child feeling selfish for wanting to do things for herself, as she is unaware of her inherent worth.

Given the long-lasting effects of childhood emotional neglect, it is necessary to use mindfulness exercises that focus on healing from emotional neglect during the reconciliation process with your inner child. The overarching purpose of mindfulness and mindful meditation is to allow the practitioner to focus on different aspects of the healing process. Within this chapter, you will be led through mindfulness meditations, each specified for one of three purposes: letting go of inner child wounds, working with difficult emotions, and learning to regulate overwhelming emotions.

Emotional neglect can occur in various ways in a child's formative years, causing damage far into adulthood if not addressed. While challenging, overcoming childhood emotional neglect is possible if you are willing to listen to your inner child and empathize with her pain.

Before covering the three mindful meditations discussed in this chapter, it is also important to understand the stages of the healing process for your neglected inner child. While the techniques in this chapter will focus on mindfulness meditations to accept that your narcissistic mother failed you emotionally, there are further steps you can take with your mindfulness meditations. Part one of the stages of healing, including the exercises within this chapter, can be worked through on your own to help you accept that your mother failed you.

It is worth noting that more intensive practices are ideally performed in the presence of a mental health professional as opposed to by yourself. Though not extensively covered in this book, parts two and three of the recovery process are still important steps for many daughters recovering from emotional neglect (Webb, 2019). Part two of healing will help you identify how your mother failed to meet your emotional needs, while part three focuses on identifying how childhood emotional neglect has influenced your adulthood. Because you will want to discuss these stages with your therapist, we will focus on mindful meditations applicable to the first stage of healing and the three functions of mindfulness.

To begin addressing the wounds leftover from childhood emotional neglect, I encourage you to glance at the following questions. These questions, provided by Jonice Webb (2019), are useful for accomplishing stage one of recovery from childhood emotional neglect. Answer the prompts as best as possible and with as much detail as you can recall.

Describe a day in your childhood at any stage. Go through the day in your mind and list the feelings you had at that time.

Write a story about your childhood when your parents supported you. Describe how they supported you in their actions and words.

Think of a time when you felt understood in your childhood by someone in your life. Were you surprised by this feeling? How did you respond to feeling heard?

✎

How did your parents express their emotions through words? For example, did your mother use words like "sad, angry, happy, scared," etc.? How freely did your mother discuss her emotions and show vulnerability?

✎

Do you recall a time when you needed your mother to nurture you, but she was not there for you? Describe this time.

✎

Seek a list of emotions and write down the ones you most identify with when recalling your memories.

✎

How Mindfulness Helps to Overcome the Wounds of Childhood Emotional Neglect

It is good to have various strategies and exercises prepared when overcoming the wounds of childhood emotional neglect. Your inner child is severely wounded because she has never been nurtured, meaning that you should attempt different practices to see what makes her feel calm and connected with you. One asset that I have always found useful is my ability to practice mindfulness and mindful meditation.

To first understand the essence of mindful meditation, it is important to know the basic functions of mindfulness when used in inner child work. These functions (Hanh, 2011) should be used as a guide when navigating mindful meditations, encouraging you to remain focused on the exercise.

The first of three mindfulness functions is using mindfulness to let go and stop fighting your inner child. Recognition, understanding, and peace with your inner child are learned during this stage. The first function of mindfulness is used early in inner child work, such as the aforementioned exercises you have learned up until now. It involves initial contact with your inner child and a brief introduction. Your promise to take care of and nurture the inner child within is formed during this function.

The second function of mindfulness is to embrace your inner child. Here, you let go of fighting your emotions and start accepting your wounded inner child for everything she is and will be. This function is the part of inner child work that helps build self-care practices as you begin taking better care of your inner child and, therefore, yourself as well. You become your inner child's closest ally and offer her nurturing and tenderness that she needs to heal.

The last function of mindfulness is learning how to soothe and relieve ourselves from difficult emotions. Given the heavy nature of inner child work, it is important to use mindfulness as a grounding tool that helps you and your inner child recollect yourself before moving forward. Here is where you soothe your inner child, taking gentle care of her as though you are gently cradling her in your arms and soothing her emotions. Mindfulness helps develop one's ability to understand the root of their pain by embracing powerful emotions. You can begin healing together by identifying the root causes of your inner child's pain.

Even if you have some experience with practicing mindfulness, it is important to know how you can implement mindfulness into your life in a way that specifically targets healing your inner child. The following exercises focus on mindfulness, with different techniques offered to help you use mindfulness to build communication and trust with your inner child. I have provided three brief meditations, each suited to a specific function of mindfulness. After going through each meditation, there will be a space for you to jot down your thoughts, emotions, and realizations after a meditation session.

Mindfulness Meditation #1: Mindfulness for Letting Go

This meditation is an example of how mindfulness serves its first purpose: letting go and refusing to fight your emotions from childhood wounds anymore. Letting go of the past with your inner child does not mean disregarding your experiences entirely–it is quite the opposite. Inner child work validates your experiences and your wounded inner child, and "letting go" of the past is a process of acceptance and moving forward.

Below is a step-by-step guide for mindfulness meditation to let go of the past, written by John Rettger (2019). Use this meditation if you feel overwhelmed during inner child work. Following the meditation will be a brief writing prompt before moving on to the second mindfulness meditation.

1. Find a comfortable, quiet area where you can be alone. Sit in a comfortable position and begin focusing on your breathing.

2. As you breathe in, feel the air coursing through your lungs–the essence of life. When you exhale, feel the emotions and thoughts slowly leaving your body.

3. Once you feel settled into a comfortable breathing pattern, recall a memory from your childhood. Your first time doing this meditation should prioritize a smaller wound you are ready to let go of. You can move on to heavier subjects or occurrences as you continue practicing.

4. As you navigate this memory, note how your body feels. Any images, physical sensations, emotions, thoughts, etc. that you feel are important to the experience.

5. Painful memories from the past often manifest into physical symptoms. While you recall this event from your childhood, your muscles may tense and tighten. Additionally, your breathing pattern may change. If this happens, remember your breathing techniques. Breathe the life into your lungs and let go of the pain your inner child is holding on to.

6. If you like, you can pause here to record anything you noticed during the meditation. While this pause is not required to have the full experience, it is helpful if you need a short break or wish to track the memory you have seen in more detail.

7. Begin looking inward again and asking yourself and your inner child some important questions. For instance, how did this event impact your future? Did any similar events during this time similarly inflict wounds on your inner child? Did you feel your inner child during the memory?

8.   Does this memory impact your feelings about yourself and your inner child? Has this instance influenced your worldview in any way?

9.   Repeat this process if you are comfortable continuing.

Below, you can fill out some more brief thoughts about this meditation. At this stage, I often list the thoughts and emotions that came to me during the meditation. Ideally, the memory will offer you insight into the past struggles and emotions your inner child is clinging to in the present. After writing these down, I move on to write opposite phrases to challenge my inner child's belief system. Remember that your inner child is still operating from a place of hurt, still suffering from negative self-talk and emotional trauma. You must listen to the inner child's feelings during inner child work. For example, if your inner child expresses guilt at this stage, you might reassure her that what happened was not her fault and that she is worthy of better treatment.

Consider writing down these challenging phrases to begin releasing your inner child's pain. You may also consider writing down things that you want to change in the future, your healing goals, etc. Anything that comes to your mind after this meditation should be jotted down.

✎

Mindfulness Meditation #2: Mindfulness for Working With Difficult Emotions

The second mindfulness meditation, provided by Carley Hauck (2018), prioritizes the healing power of mindfulness when you are tackling difficult, painful emotions and memories. The second function of mindfulness works to help you accept your inner child and all the negative emotions that you have grown used to pushing away. Ideally, you will now begin accepting your inner child for who she is and everything she feels–however, once you do this, you will need to have mindfulness practices aimed at addressing overwhelming emotions. This meditation takes around ten minutes, making it perfect for people with a tight schedule.

1.   Begin this meditation in a comfortable, seated position. Close your eyes if you would like. Imagine a difficult experience or emotion you and your inner child are facing. As you recognize this feeling, also recognize your instinct to push the feeling away. Think of your desire to shove negative feelings out of sight and turn towards unhealthy coping methods to soothe your pain.

2.   Once you have recognized harmful temptations, turn toward them. Overcoming our negative habits during inner child healing work is only possible if you are willing to embrace everything your inner child feels, even the negative.

3. Breathe deeply, in through your nose and out through your mouth. Do this a few times until you reach a state of calm.

4. Bring into awareness a motherly, nurturing figure–in the case of inner child healing, this should be your adult self. This woman should be someone compassionate, loving, and trusting. Feel her as she wraps her arms around your inner child, enveloping her in a blanket of love, warmth, acceptance, and safety.

5. Continue picturing the motherly figure cradling you in her arms and the protection she offers.

6. Next, completely turn toward the difficult emotion you are facing. As you do this, hear the woman cradling you, telling you that everything will be alright and that you are safe. Nothing bad will happen in the circle of her arms, and she will stand by your inner child's side and offer protection.

7. Picture the woman giving you words of encouragement and solidarity. As you face your emotion, keep hearing these words, allowing yourself to receive loving, kind words until you feel your mind and body calming down.

8. Whenever you feel yourself turning away from the difficult emotion, take a few deep breaths and try to shift your attention back to the issue gently. It will not always be comfortable, but

being able to face things head-on is crucial to communicating with your inner child.

9. Hold on to a grounding object during this meditation if it makes you feel comforted and protected, such as a stone, keepsake, or any object that calms you.

Below, you can fill out your thoughts after this meditation. Write down in your journal any emotions, messages, or sensations you have after completing this exercise.

✎

Additionally, feel free to answer any of the following:

Does how you feel after the meditation challenge how you felt before?

✎

Did you gain any valuable insights from your inner child?

✎

What troubling emotion would you eventually want to address with this meditation?

✎

Mindfulness Meditation #3: Mindfulness for Regulating Emotions

This final meditation will prioritize the third function of mindfulness: learning to regulate your emotions. Some individuals struggle to regulate emotions because regulation may get confused with repression. This is not the case. Allow yourself to feel what you feel and do not fight your emotions. However, one of the issues with extreme, overwhelming emotions is that people often turn to harmful methods to cope with their emotions. Instead, you must learn techniques to work with your emotions and calmly address what troubles you. Below is a brief mindfulness meditation created by Paul Harrison (2015), aimed at emotional regulation.

1. Find a quiet spot where you have privacy. Sit in a comfortable position with good posture and close your eyes.

2. Set a timer for ten minutes.

3. Begin to focus on your breathing. Breathe in whatever way feels most natural and fulfilling to you. As your breath moves through your body, feel how it lights up every part of you. Stay settled on your breathing.

4. As you continue focusing on your breathing, also start noticing any emotions or thoughts that come to you.

5. Do not fight any emotions that come to you. This is a denial of your inner child's pain. Instead, sit with the emotions and simply let them exist–do not fight or indulge.

6. Now, start observing the emotion. How does it feel? Do you feel its energy inside of you?

7. Name this emotion.

8. As you breathe, let go of this emotion on an exhale, feeling the energy and negativity exit your lungs as you inhale peace and calm. It is normal to get emotional during this meditation–if that is the case, allow yourself to cry and understand how you feel while handling your emotions mindfully.

Below is another space for you to write any thoughts you have post-meditation. For instance, consider the emotion you identified. How have you struggled to regulate it before? Do you feel like you can regulate it now? How did your inner child feel as you let that negativity go?

⋯⋯•⋅•⋅⋅⋅

Healing the wounds leftover from your mother's emotional neglect is possible if you work with your inner child to practice mindfulness and offer her support during every step of the healing journey. The upcoming chapter will make it easier to identify the signs of your wounded inner child to take a step closer to healing the open neglect wounds that you have ignored for years. By opening yourself up to identifying the signs of your hidden inner child, you can navigate the healing process with a straightforward understanding of what your inner child needs from you.

Chapter Four

Identifying the Signs of Your Wounded Inner Child

L EARNING TO COMMUNICATE WITH your inner child requires you to understand how inner child wounds manifest
in your adult life. Daughters of narcissistic abuse often downplay
their childhood experiences and lessen the impact of their mother's
abusive behavior. Because of this, ignoring inner child wounds has
become second nature for you.

This chapter will prioritize exercises that help you identify the
signs of your wounded inner child. Knowing the signs of inner
child wounds will help you understand the best way to nurture
and care for your wounded inner child.

To begin, consult the checklist below to identify signs that your inner child needs to heal. Check off any listed signs of a wounded inner child.

- You struggle to convince yourself that the abuse you endured was not your fault.
- You have low self-esteem and compare yourself to others.
- You react more extremely than others at minor inconveniences.
- You struggle to trust others and still carry the mindset instilled by your mother that you cannot trust anyone but her.
- You have codependent tendencies and often jump into relationships and place your trust in someone straight away.
- You doubt your emotions and seek outside validation.
- You fear conflict and try to avoid it whenever possible.
- You have unhealthy coping mechanisms.
- You sabotage healthy relationships because you fear being hurt or think you are undeserving of happiness.
- You struggle to say no to requests from people around you.
- You often fear the possibility of being abandoned by another person.
- You hide things from others and are evasive.
- You are overly self-critical over small mistakes.
- You are afraid of the future and the unknown.

····•··•····

Once you have identified signs of your wounded inner child, it becomes easier to discover how you can help her heal. Determining how your wounded inner child influences your adult self can uncover everything that your inner child has hidden from you. All the pain, grief and fear that you have pushed away in the past exists within her, and by recognizing these signs, you and her can take another step towards healing.

It is important to understand *why* your inner child hides her wounds from you. As you may recall from the guide, your inner child holds all the shame remaining from your childhood trauma. All of your childhood experiences and wounds are kept locked away by your inner child in an attempt to prevent you from facing the full force of your pain. As you work with her to identify the wounds she is hiding from you, you will be able to process lingering pain from your childhood trauma and heal your inner child.

Though your wounded inner child does not intentionally cause you harm, leaving her trauma unresolved causes significant damage to your mental health as an adult. By practicing exercises aimed at identifying the signs of your wounded inner child, you can begin learning about the pain she hides from you.

Exercise to Find Your Inner Child

This exercise helps practitioners look deep within to find their inner child. Many people falsely assume that their inner child is nonexistent because they have lost contact with their child self. Letting go of this superstition and acknowledging the existence and validity of your wounded inner child is integral to your healing.

This exercise, inspired by an exercise written by Zuzu Perkal (n.d.), involves daydreaming as a technique for contacting your inner child successfully. Following the initial daydreaming outline are short journal questions to help process your findings. Finally, you will be provided with a supplementary exercise that works best when done after the initial daydreaming exercise.

To begin this exercise, find a comfortable place where you can be alone. Close your eyes and take deep breaths, inhaling through your nose and exhaling through your mouth until you have found a comfortable rhythm. Start thinking back to your childhood and what it felt like to be a child. As the daughter of a narcissistic mother, these feelings are often unpleasant and painful. Identify some of the emotions you feel as you reflect on your childhood. Without losing focus on the image of your childhood, try to think of emotions that you would associate with childhood with other people in general.

Focus on a specific part of your childhood and what you felt during this time. As you allow yourself to recall the past, begin thinking about what your inner child has missed out on. Imagine her ideal childhood. Is she playing? Drawing? With friends? Consider experiences that your inner child craves, whether this is exploring different hobbies, meeting new friends, being held in her mother's arms, or anything else you feel you missed out on in your childhood.

As you determine what your inner child wants from her life, start to visualize what you are hearing. If your inner child is playing outside, for instance, you may build a scene around her, starting from the ground and making your way up until you can see the entire space that your inner child is occupying. Perhaps she is at a playground, running around the slides and monkey bars and asking a friend to play on the see-saw with her. Perhaps *you* are her friend in this scene, running and playing with her and witnessing her pure, unadulterated happiness.

If your daydream is not particularly detailed, it does not mean that you have failed. Continue trying to shift your focus to this scene and notice as many details as you can, even if they seem irrelevant.

Once you have captured your scene, you can move on to the journaling portion of this exercise. Below are some questions about your daydream, such as what you witnessed and your contact with your inner child. You can also use these questions as prompts to create a journal entry about your experience.

1.   Within your daydream, you came into brief contact with your inner child. What did you feel towards her? What did you love about her?

2.   Did you feel happy at any point during this exercise? If so, what about your daydream brought you happiness?

3.   What was life like for your inner child? Did she carry the same burdens that you did at her age, or was she more playful and carefree? What is important to her?

4.   What did you hope to express to your inner child during this exercise? Did you communicate your thoughts with her? Whether or not you were able to communicate with her, what do you want to share with her in the future?

5. What do you hope your inner child will have in the future? Do you envision her story as a rewrite of your childhood and what you wanted from life at the time? How can you ensure that your inner child will receive the care she needs to develop?

✎

As you consider these questions, keep an open mind and write down whatever thoughts flow into your consciousness. If you see any other images, take note of these as well. Now, you can move on to the supplementary exercise below. This exercise can be done independently, but I find it most effective when I do it after my initial daydreaming and journaling.

Taking the Initiative: Describe Your Inner Child

Often, you will uncover various facts about your wounded inner child through simple practices. This exercise, while perhaps less intense and involved than other exercises, still offers significant insights into the life of your inner child. In the following exercises, you will be encouraged to list words about your inner child, divided into three parts of speech: adjectives, nouns, and verbs.

In the lists below, I have provided some examples of words you may use to describe your inner child. Check off three adjectives that you feel are most accurate in describing your inner child. Do not think too hard about why you resonate most with these words–simply pick what feels right to you.

Adjectives to Describe Your Inner Child

- Brave
- Happy
- Loving
- Generous
- Polite
- Calm
- Cautious
- Carefree
- Eager
- Hopeful
- Fragile
- Hurt
- Kind
- Lonely
- Powerful
- Shy
- Wide-eyed
- Giving
- Sensible
- Ambitious
- Independent
- Loyal
- Wise

Nouns to Describe Your Inner Child

Now, go through the same process again, this time choosing the three nouns that best describe your inner child and how she sees herself in relation to others.

- Daughter
- Sister
- Caretaker
- Mitigator
- Rebel
- Fighter
- Friend
- Leader
- Follower
- Mother
- Passenger
- Teacher
- Baby
- Skeptic
- Believer
- Student
- Novice
- Adult
- Outlier
- Worker
- Artist

- Individual
- Conformist

Verbs to Describe Your Inner Child

Finally, the below list will offer verbs that you can use to describe your inner child. With these words, consider activities or actions that you associate with your inner child. Some of the words may describe activities that you think your inner child may have enjoyed, while you may associate other words with your inner child's instinctual responses to external conditions. Again, select the three words that resonate most with you.

- Appeal
- Avoid
- Become
- Adapt
- Argue
- Play
- Believe
- Behave
- Give
- Listen
- Hide
- Quit
- Rely
- Try

- Wish
- Win
- Lose
- Tell
- Survive
- Regret
- Observe
- Compete
- Need

As you go through these lists, you may feel like more than three of the words listed resonate with you and your inner child. While you might be tempted to select more than three words, part of your healing will require that you understand your inner child on a deeply personal level. By limiting yourself to selecting only three words from each section, you are investing more time and effort into getting to know your inner child. Selecting a smaller number of words helps you get into the granular details of the wounds that your inner child suffers from.

· · · · ● · ● · · · ·

In the earlier stages of healing my wounded inner child, I found that one of the most unnerving aspects of this journey was that I did not know what to expect from my inner child. I knew that she was hurting and that she needed me to be there for her, but

I could not imagine our conversations in great detail. This was deeply frustrating to me because while I knew that my inner child had pure intentions, I could not figure out how to communicate with her in a way that reassured her of my gentle love.

Inner child work will bring up memories that you have spent years ignoring or forgetting. The process involves concentration and introspection, along with a true dedication to nurturing and loving your inner child. As you become a parental figure to your inner child, communication will come more naturally. During my initial journey, writing was one of my most valued assets to express my feelings and apprehensions to my inner child. Below is another example of a letter you may consider writing to your inner child.

This letter is specifically meant for the earlier stages of inner child healing, though you can write similar letters at any stage of your journey when you feel out of sync with her. After the example, I have listed some questions that are key to connecting with your inner child and learning what to expect from her.

Dear Inner Child,

I am writing once again to speak honestly to you. I know that communication is something that can be scary for both of us, but I want to keep trying until we are both comfortable in one another's presence. I trust that whatever you have to say to me is honest and valid, and while I don't know exactly what to expect from our healing journey, I know that we can get through anything together.

I feel excited about the prospect of healing, though I often get caught up in irrational worries about its effectiveness. However, I still do not know what you want from me and what you need from this journey. Because of that, I encourage you to speak your mind candidly whenever you are ready. For now, I will tell you what I am hoping for from the path ahead of us.

During this process, I want to know everything about you. I imagine that you have various passions and interests that I have forgotten about over the years, and I hope to share these interests with you when you are ready to take that step. I am also aware of the painful memories that you hold, and while uncovering these memories is frightening in many ways, I know that we will be fine if we commit ourselves to the process. I expect that you will be honest with me once I have shown you my dedication to caring for you. I hope that my actions in the future will demonstrate the honesty behind my words here.

However, I do not only want to cover what I expect from you and our journey but what you can expect from me as well. I cannot promise that the path ahead will be easy for either of us, but I can promise to nurture, love, and care for you no matter what. Whatever we discover together, I will be there to hold you and remind you of how far we have come. No matter how unexpected these revelations and memories are to me, I will not leave your side at any point in this process.

Before we continue on our path, I want to remind you that you are loved, strong, and valued. Your resilience inspires me and pushes me to continue working on our healing, no matter how rough it seems. Whether we are going through calm or choppy waters, I will be there to support and defend you every step of the way. I look forward to communicating with you again and showing you the depth of my love.

Sincerely,

Your Adult Self

· · · · ● · ● · · · ·

To conclude this chapter, I have provided a brief list of questions that you can ask yourself before writing a new letter to your inner child. Your goal with these questions is to gain a better understanding of what you and your inner child should expect from one another.

What words do you want to be able to describe yourself with once you have completed the initial process of accepting and communicating with your inner child? ✎

What do you *think* your inner child wants from you? What do you want from her?

✎

Going back to the adjectives, nouns, and verbs portion of this chapter, are there any words you selected for your inner child that surprise you? If so, why do you think these words resonated with your inner child?

✎

What is your biggest worry about inner child work? Does your inner child share this worry?

✎

What do you expect from inner child work in general? For instance, are there specific emotions, events, roadblocks, or exercises you anticipate from inner child work?

✎

Chapter Five

Uncovering Your Authentic Self

IN THE GUIDE, THE topic of the authentic self as it relates to your inner child was heavily discussed. Growing up as the scapegoat daughter of a narcissistic mother causes you to lose sight of your authentic self. Because you were not given the freedom to express your true self as a child, uncovering your authentic self during inner child work is a daunting task.

Rediscovering your authentic self requires reconciliation with your inner child. Your inner child's authentic self will offer valuable insights on your healing path moving forward. To start understanding your authentic self, this chapter will guide you through exercises aimed at identifying key attributes of your wounded inner child and how her individuality has been lost over the years. By doing this, you can continue learning about what your inner child needs from you as a parental figure.

Exercise to Align Your Authentic Inner Child and Adult Self

Below is the first part of a two-part exercise where you will be encouraged through prompts to recall specific childhood memories. Take your time and return to any questions that seem too heavy at the moment–however, you must commit yourself to come back to these questions and answer them when you are prepared. You will find various prompts to help you return to your childhood. Take your time to answer these questions in as much detail as possible.

As a kid, what did you want to be when you grew up?

What were your favorite games to play as a child?

Did you have any favorite/treasured toys when you were young?

Who did you feel safest with as a child?

What were your childhood dreams for the future? At what stage did you begin losing these dreams?

✎

In as much detail as possible, describe your happiest childhood memory.

✎

Did you have a favorite place to be as a child?

✎

What was a typical day in your childhood like?

✎

As a child, how would you describe your mother in a few words?

✎

If you have siblings, what was your relationship with them like as a child?

✎

What can you remember about your childhood home?

✎

What is your earliest memory?

✎

What were your friends like during your childhood? Describe them in a few words.

✎

Did your family ascribe to any religious or otherwise spiritual beliefs? How did this impact your childhood and family life?

✎

Once you have answered the questions above and feel ready to continue, move on to the prompts below. These prompts are about your adulthood and any similarities or differences between you and your child self. Answer as honestly as possible, taking short breaks when needed.

What is your profession as an adult? Is it the same or similar to the profession you wanted as a child?

✎

What hobbies do you enjoy most? Did you have similar hobbies in your childhood?

✎

What activities did you do in your childhood that you wish you could revisit as an adult?

✎

Who do you feel safest around as an adult? ✎

What hopes and dreams do you have for the future? Are these similar to what you dreamed of as a child?

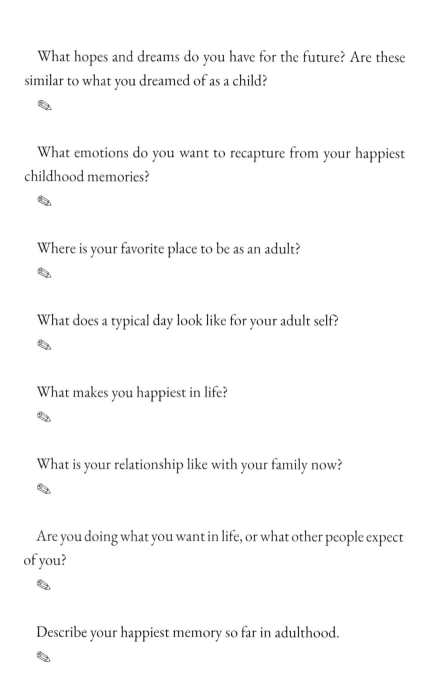

What emotions do you want to recapture from your happiest childhood memories?

Where is your favorite place to be as an adult?

What does a typical day look like for your adult self?

What makes you happiest in life?

What is your relationship like with your family now?

Are you doing what you want in life, or what other people expect of you?

Describe your happiest memory so far in adulthood.

Do you feel like you are honest with yourself and living according to your values?

✎

What feels right to you in your life? This can include the people around you, your profession, your hobbies, etc.

✎

After answering these questions, reflect on any similarities and differences you notice between the first and second parts of this exercise. Ultimately, your truest self is found within your inner child. By comparing your answers in the above prompts with one another, you can see how your inner child aligns with your adult self. Additionally, any drastic differences you notice between the two sets of prompts can offer insight into how burying your childhood wounds and trauma has affected you in your adult life.

Exercise to Know Who You Are

Despite how simple it sounds, one question plagues many people throughout their lives: who am I? It is a short question that requires a long answer and frequent introspection. Along with this, it is a question that is key to healing your wounded inner child. Though one exercise alone cannot tell you everything that you need to know about yourself and your inner child, the following questions will help you build a foundation for understanding your authentic self. This two-part exercise (Sutton, 2021) will help guide you through important questions to ask yourself to truly optimize your inner child's healing experience.

Part One: Who Am I?

Building your self-awareness through careful introspection is crucial to uncovering your authentic self. By starting to figure out who you are, you can solidify a relationship with your inner child and build a sturdy foundation to continue discovering yourself.

Answer the questions below in as much detail as possible, being as candid as you can be. This exercise is best done in a quiet place where you can take time to truly think and reflect without worrying about other people in the space. When answering these questions, do not cast judgment upon yourself, and remember that there is no right or wrong way to respond. Your answers are for you and your inner child, not for anyone else, and you should remind yourself of that whenever you are hesitant about one of your answers.

The people in our lives, for better or worse, commonly view us differently from how we view ourselves. Looking at yourself from a new perspective can shine a light on who you are at your core and who you want to be. Because of this, the first three questions below focus on understanding yourself through the eyes of those closest to you.

1.　How would those closest to you describe you in one paragraph? What would your friends or family say if they were sharing their unfiltered thoughts about you?

2.　Imagine someone at work telling a new coworker a story about you. What story would they tell?

3.　Picture your life partner describing you to other people. How would they describe your life? What would they mention about you in a biography?

Part Two: Debriefing

Once you have considered and answered the previous questions, you can move on to the final step of this exercise: the debrief. This section will also encourage you to answer questions, this time based on how you responded in part one. You can answer these questions in your journal if you wish to write out your thoughts in more detail. When you are ready, ask yourself the following:

What stands out most about my answers?

✎

What, if anything, surprises me with my answers?

✎

How do I feel now that I have completed part one of this exercise?

✎

What have I learned by looking at myself through the eyes of another?

✎

How can I continue to foster self-awareness?

✎

Creating Your Mission Statement

Understanding your authentic self and reconnecting with your inner child is most successful when you have an overall mission in mind. Because of this, having an exercise aimed at creating your mission statement is important to help you mentor your inner child with compassion and knowledge.

This exercise (Sutton, 2021) will help you create a mission statement to clarify what you stand for and what you hope to achieve in your life. You will begin by answering key questions to help inform your mission statement. Then, you will take your findings to create a complete, thorough mission statement that will guide you through the rest of your inner child work.

1.   What is the most important thing to me in life?

2.   What do I consider to be my key values?

3.   What am I most passionate about?

4.   What are my current personal and professional goals?

5.   What do I envision when I think of the best version of myself? Is there a specific job, relationship, or life goal that I associate with the best version of myself?

6.   What do other people consider my greatest strengths?

7. What legacy do I want to leave behind, and what skills will help me achieve this legacy?

✐

Now, take the most important aspects of these answers to create your mission statement. If you are not sure how to create a mission statement, you can follow this format and the example provided.

_I will _____ (action) for_____ (audience) by _____ (skills) to _____ (desired outcome)._

For example, in the context of inner child healing, your mission statement may look something like this:

I will help nurture and care for my wounded inner child by practicing inner child healing exercises every day to reach a state of total healing and connection with her.

Write your personal mission statement below.

✐

·········

As you work on discovering your authentic self, you may find yourself feeling vulnerable or insecure. Because you have spent so many years hiding your inner child, finding her once again and coming to terms with your truest self is not only challenging, but frightening. While feeling vulnerable during this process is natural, you can start overcoming these insecurities through positive affirmations.

Below are numerous affirmations that you can use while discovering your authentic self. Whenever you find your mind clouded by self-doubt, you can return to these affirmations to quell any anxieties you and your inner child are facing. Feel free to highlight or otherwise mark any affirmations that speak to you.

1. I have the power to get through anything life throws my way.
2. I am worthy of love and compassion.
3. I am not at fault for the abuse others have pushed upon me.
4. I am not alone.
5. I am surrounded and fulfilled by love from myself and others.
6. I choose myself every day.
7. I have made it through my worst and lowest moments. I will survive and proceed with resilience in everything I do.

8. I no longer feel guilty or ashamed of my childhood experiences.

9. I am valuable, and I determine my value.

10. I deserve respect, just like anyone else.

11. My worthiness cannot be defined by others. I am inherently worthy.

12. My inner child is a powerful, unyielding force.

13. I love and nurture myself every day.

14. I am at peace.

15. I accept every part of myself.

16. I know my truth and will not let other people deny what I know to be a fact.

17. I believe in myself no matter what happens.

18. My childhood trauma does not define me.

19. I practice self-care to nurture my inner child.

20. I am never alone.

21. I do not owe my abusers forgiveness.

22. I am powerful.

23. I have a bright future ahead of me.

24. I make progress every single day.

25. I will continue to heal alongside my inner child.

26. I know that total healing is possible.

27. I do not second-guess the compliments other people give me.

28. I am a lovable person.

29. I do my best no matter what, and failures do not define me.

30. I deserve to have my boundaries understood and respected by other people.

31. I can achieve whatever I hope to in life.

32. I am in charge.

33. I do not measure my worth by comparing myself to others.

34. Struggling with my emotions does not make me weak.

35. I am safe.

36. I have a greater purpose.

37. I do not second-guess myself.

38. I can recognize unhealthy relationship patterns.

39. I protect myself and my inner child, no matter what.

40. My feelings, even the negative ones, are valid.

41. I know everything will work out.

42. I am brave.

43. I am where I need to be in my life.

44. I focus on what I can control instead of what I cannot.

45. I am grateful for the many blessings in my life.

Bringing Your Authentic Self into Adulthood

Finding small ways to bring out your authentic self as an adult is essential to your overall progress in this journey. Because your authentic self is stored in your inner child, connecting with her allows you to connect with every aspect of your being. However, in the same way that it takes time to discover your inner child, learning about your authentic self takes time and practice. Starting with small exercises will help you build your communication skills with your authentic self and inner child.

One simple way that you can begin bringing your authentic self into adulthood is by incorporating some of your favorite childhood activities into your daily life. For instance, if you enjoyed drawing or coloring as a child, you may consider picking up the habit again as an adult. Additionally, you may consider revisiting places that brought you comfort as a child, whether this is a friend's home, a library, or anywhere else that calms your inner child.

You might also consider trying out new hobbies that your inner child never got a chance to explore. Any activities, passions, or adventures that were forgotten because of your mother can now be rediscovered as an adult. Part of reconnecting with your wounded inner child is remembering that your shared past does not define you.

Your inner child is her own person, worthy of nurturing and respect from people in her life. By exploring new interests and opening yourself up to the possibilities, you will find peace with your inner child and explore new, exciting moments with her.

To conclude this chapter, I have provided you with a simple template to start practicing new hobbies and exploring your inner child's interests. For each day of the week, I have offered a potential activity as an example of your new schedule. Additionally, you will find a blank space to plan your chosen activity for a well-rounded week.

Day of the Week: *Monday*

Possible Activity: *Journal about what I want to accomplish this week*

What I Will Do Today: ✎

Day of the Week: *Tuesday*

Possible Activity: *Make my favorite childhood meal*

What I Will Do Today: ✎

Day of the Week: *Wednesday*

Possible Activity: *Practice drawing again*

What I Will Do Today: ✎

Day of the Week: *Thursday*

Possible Activity: *Take part in a new sport or activity*

What I Will Do Today: ✎

Day of the Week: *Friday*

Possible Activity: *Meet up with a childhood friend*

What I Will Do Today: ✎

Day of the Week: *Saturday*

Possible Activity: *Go to my inner child's favorite local spot*

What I Will Do Today: ✎

Day of the Week: *Sunday*

Possible Activity: *Write a letter to my inner child about the week we have had*

What I Will Do Today: ✎

Chapter Six

Going Through the Stages

H EALING YOUR INNER CHILD requires not only you to acknowledge that the wounds are there but also for you to be willing to go back to specific points in your childhood where you were wounded. Because there are numerous points where you sustained wounds–including some that you have likely forgotten–understanding your inner child's pain is simpler when you can break your childhood down into separate stages.

As described in the *Inner Child Healing Guide*, the seven stages of childhood covered here are: newborn, early infancy, infancy, preschool age, junior school age, secondary school age, and high school age. During each of these stages, your inner child was wounded by your mother in some way. No matter how big or small the wound is, it still plagues and harms your inner child today. This chapter will guide you through exercises centered on the different stages of childhood and how to identify specific incidents where you were wounded by your narcissistic mother.

Exercise to Revisit the Past

Before you can move into more intensive exercises in this chapter, you must begin with a simple exercise to take you back to the different stages of your childhood. This exercise helps you to begin recalling the past by looking at photos of your childhood self. If you do not have enough photos for this exercise to be feasible, then you can instead use other objects from your childhood, like a favorite item, old schoolwork, or art that you made as a kid. However, I find that photos are the most effective as you move into the next step of this chapter: visualization.

Recalling your childhood memories by turning to photos or other mementos from the time is a surefire way to start getting into the same headspace as your inner child. To do this, take time out of your day to go through old photographs. If you have a photo album of childhood memories, flip through the album's pages and see how you have grown over the years. Ideally, you will be able to find photos from different stages of your childhood to see how you progressed over the years.

School yearbooks are also a great source if you do not have enough photos from your childhood or simply want to add another element to this exercise. If you have any writings from your childhood, such as a diary, then reading through these pages is yet another way of understanding the mindset that your inner child still has.

As you go through your mementos, gather as much information as you can about the child you see. If you are looking at a photo album, recall when each picture was taken and any memories or emotions you associate with that picture. If you are looking through a school yearbook, consider the age that you were at the time, who you were surrounded by during your education, or any memorable images or emotions that the photo arouses. As you go through any writings from your childhood, take time to study the words and the way that you expressed yourself as a child. In this instance, you can compare your childhood diary entries with your current journal entries to identify any significant differences in the examples.

It is best to try to find as many mementos as you can from your childhood when you are practicing this exercise. Doing this will help your inner child feel more comfortable in showing herself to you, and finding things that connect with her will foster communication between you.

While not required, it may be helpful to jot down some notes about specific mementos as you go through the ones you find. For instance, if you find a picture that brings up certain emotions, thoughts, or memories, you can jot down a quick note about what you feel in your journal or on the back of the image. This is particularly helpful if you are going through numerous mementos.

Visualizations for the Seven Stages of Childhood

Once you have gotten back into the headspace of your inner child by enlisting the help of childhood mementos, you can start practicing different visualizations to expand on your unlocked memories. This section will go through visualizations specifically tailored to different stages of your childhood, going into greater detail as the exercises progress. While you may need to take some creative liberties for the first two stages where you may not have concrete memories, further stages will go into more detail. Additionally, try to use your mementos during these visualizations. While not required, your mementos can help you immerse yourself in the memories that your inner child is storing.

Visualization for Stage One: Newborn

Find a comfortable, quiet place where you can sit alone without disruptions. Visualizations for the stages of childhood are most effective when you do not have time constraints or any pressing events you must make that day. There is no concrete time for how long visualizations last, so it is important that you do not feel the need to rush yourself through the process.

While breathing in through your nose and out through your mouth, start to close your eyes. Focus on the sound and the sensation of your breathing, paying close attention to how your chest expands with every inhale and contracts with every exhale. Let the room around you melt away, focusing only on your breathing. Once you fall into a comfortable rhythm, begin building a scene around you.

Place yourself in your childhood bedroom, recalling as many details as you can. Pay attention to the color of your walls, any toys strewn about, or any sounds you notice. Now, envision a crib in the center of the room. If you know what your crib looked like, then you can imagine this; if not, simply envision another crib. In the crib lies a newborn baby, no more than two weeks old. She is lying on her back, eyes closed, her chest moving up and down as she breathes. She is sleeping, but small sounds emanate from her, as though she is dreaming about something but does not have the words to express it yet.

Add more details to the child, as many as you can. For instance, notice what she is wearing, the small whispers of hair on her head, her gentle exhales, her fists curling into balls like she is learning to grab things as she rests. Notice what you feel towards this child. Compassion? Love? Regret? Sadness? Whatever you feel, allow your emotions to wash over you.

Picture the child beginning to become restless. Imagine that she begins to cry, waiting for the nurturing love of her mother. While she does not know who the mother is yet, she still calls out for her. This newborn is your inner child, calling out to be nurtured, to be loved, to be cared for. Your mother never comes, and your inner child continues to cry.

Now, envision yourself gently reaching into the crib and lifting your inner child out. Cradle her against your chest, carefully holding her in your arms and slowly rocking her back and forth. Feel how you are connected with her at this moment. Words do not need to be said at this point; the comforting touch of a mother is enough for your inner child. Care for her as you would with any newborn baby, giving her gentleness and compassion that she has not yet experienced.

Though your inner child cannot reply, you will want to leave her with a few words before you depart this visualization. Notice how your inner child falls asleep in the safety of your arms. She may not know you yet, but she has started to trust you. Once she has gone back to sleep, place your inner child back in her crib, making sure that she is safe and comfortable. Tell her words of reassurance and love. *I love you, I will never leave you, I will always be here for you, and I will take care of you no matter what.*

Slowly come back to the space you are currently occupying. Envision yourself exiting through your inner child's bedroom door and back into your room, gently opening your eyes and taking in your surroundings. Continue to breathe deeply, in and out, using your breath as a grounding tool. If possible, turn to one of the mementos that you had during the newborn stage, such as an image or a stuffed animal. For instance, I may choose to look at a picture of myself from when I was first born at the hospital. When I do this, I tell my younger self: *You are loved, and you are valued. I will take care of you every step of the way. You will never be alone in this world.*

Visualization for Stage Two: Early Infancy

Early infancy begins once the child is one month old up until their first birthday. While this is another period of your childhood that you might not remember, you can still use visualizations to truly connect with your inner child. Right now, you are taking on the position of a mother for your inner child. By doing visualizations of your inner child at such a young age, you can grow with her, making it possible to understand her and yourself.

This visualization will begin in the same way that the first visualization and the remainder of the visualizations do. Finding a quiet and comfortable space, sit and close your eyes. Focus on your breathing, noticing any sensations in your body as the air courses through, bringing you life. Do your best to ignore any outside noises or stressors, giving your full attention to your breathing. If you find your mind wandering, gently shift it back to your breath and focus on your visualization.

Now, begin to build the scene in your mind. This time, picture your inner child at the age of six months. She has just begun gaining more motor skills and is learning to crawl. As she lies on a blanket, she tries to pick herself up and move her body forward. As she rocks back and forth, making little progress, her face begins to grow frustrated. She bounces on her knees, trying to move but unable to without guidance.

As your inner child continues to attempt crawling, begin building the space around her. Where is she now? Is she in the living room of your childhood home? Is she at a family member's house? Is she somewhere that you consider a safe space?

Now, begin moving towards your inner child, kneeling on the ground next to her. While she needs help learning how to crawl, she has not been offered guidance from anyone. Your nurturing, loving lessons are exactly what she needs right now. Feel the carpet beneath your hands and knees, and as you kneel next to your inner child, imagine that you are her, that this is a new experience for you, too.

While watching your inner child, begin to move on your knees, one hand in front of the other, as a crawling child would. After moving a few steps forward, look back at your inner child. Watch how she bounces on her knees, trying to follow in your footsteps. Turn your body towards her and hold out your arms.

Begin encouraging your inner child. *You've got this. You can do it. You can do anything you set your mind to.* Keeping your arms open, watch as your inner child slowly begins to make progress towards you, inching forward, trying to follow your lead. Once she has reached you, scoop her up in your arms and hold her close. Comfort her in whatever way you feel is most effective, such as gently running your hand over her head, kissing her forehead, or nuzzling against her cheek. Everything that you do should be done with pure, honest love. Lay her down on her stomach after you hold her and watch as she tries to get up again and crawl. Continue reassuring and motivating her, reminding her of her strength and capabilities.

As you begin to leave this space, leave your inner child with some parting words: *I am proud of you. I love you. I cannot wait to see what our future holds.*

Now, bring yourself back to the present, taking a few more deep, grounding breaths before returning to your natural rhythm. If you do not have a memento of this time to ground you, then look at the room around you, taking in as many details as possible. What colors do you see? What sounds do you hear? What objects catch your eye? What feels different about you, if anything?

Visualization for Stage Three: Infancy

Stage three of childhood occurs between the ages of one and three, marking various significant changes in a child's communication, verbal, and motor skills. However, because of the neglect daughters of narcissistic mothers face, this time in a child's life is often challenging and filled with uncertainty.

When you are ready to begin this visualization to discover unhealed inner child wounds, you can find a comfortable space and let your breath fall into a calming rhythm. As you move on to this meditation, keep in mind that you do not have to complete all of these visualizations in rapid succession–these exercises are meant to bring you peace and relaxation, not stress you out. If necessary, take a break from the room you are in and relocate, or journal about what you are feeling after your previous visualizations. If you need to wait for a different day to be mentally prepared to move forward, that is okay–so long as you still commit yourself to completing the visualization.

As your breathing begins to even out, allow your eyes to close. As the world melts away around you, shift your entire focus to your breathing. While breathing in through your nose and out through your mouth, begin expanding your mind, opening it to new information that you will discover during this visualization.

Once you feel fully immersed in the visualization, start picturing your inner child at about two years old. Her motor skills are beginning to improve, and she is standing right in front of the stairs, looking up to determine whether or not she is capable of climbing them. She is young, however, and headstrong, and nothing will stop her from trying. Build up the scene around her, letting more details slowly trickle into your visualization. Imagine the stairs from your childhood home or one of your favorite spots as a child. Try to develop as many details as possible to make the scene feel more realistic. Are the stairs carpeted? Wood? Tile? Is there anything notable about them, such as signs of wear? Is there a banister that your inner child can hold onto?

In this image, your inner child is alone, with seemingly no one else around her. She looks up at the stairs with some trepidation and overwhelming curiosity. Though her desire to climb the stairs is evident in her gaze, you can tell that she is hesitant. No one is around her as far as she knows, no one to catch her if she falls or congratulate her if she succeeds. Still, you can see a determined glint in her eye, one that tells you that she is going to do this, no matter how difficult the climb becomes.

Place your full attention on your inner child as she stands before the staircase. Slowly make your way towards her. Do not rush the process, as you may risk scaring her away if you do so. As you get closer to her, gently make your presence known. You may consider saying a simple introduction or asking her a question or communicating nonverbally with a wave.

If you choose to communicate verbally, keep your tone gentle and supportive. Speak to her in a low voice, allowing warmth to come through with every word. *Hello. You're doing amazing with your walking. You'll be climbing up those stairs in no time, and I will be here to cheer you on as you make this step. You can do anything you set your mind to, and no matter what path you take or what speed you learn, I will remain your biggest supporter.*

In your mind's eye, watch as your inner child lifts her leg to the first step, shaky but determined. Watch as she continues to climb and reflect on all the bravery and resilience she is exhibiting. As she continues climbing upwards, give her the loving, nurturing encouragement that she needs now. Though she is strong, she needs the love of a mother, someone who will nurture her growth and encourage healthy independence.

Watch as your inner child reaches the top of the stairs, tired from the exertion but still smiling, proud of this achievement. Speak to her once again at this stage, offering words of love and encouragement. If she does not respond to your comforting statements, that is okay–as long as she is aware of your presence, you are taking a step in the right direction. If your inner child is responding well to you and feels comfortable, you can watch as she makes her way back down the stairs or help her come back down yourself. Whether you are lending a helping hand or simply offering your inner child support, this visualization can help build trust and understanding between you and your wounded inner child.

Before departing this visualization, leave your inner child with a few words of love and encouragement. *You did amazing. I am so proud of you and how you are growing. I can't wait to see you again and support your growth in whatever way you need me to. I love you.*

Let the image slowly melt away as you bring your attention back to your breathing. Take a few more deep, steady breaths as you start to fall back into your natural rhythm. Slowly open your eyes and take in the scene around you. If you are using a memento for this visualization, hold it in your hands or close to your chest. Picture your inner child and how she struggled but persevered. Now, she does not have to face new obstacles alone. As you continue forward, you can offer your inner child the love and support that she desperately needs. While you and she are strong individually, you become an unstoppable force when you work together.

Visualization for Stage Four: Preschool Age

This visualization will cover the preschool stage of childhood, specifically from the age of three to the age of five or six. At this stage of life, a child has developed many motor and verbal skills and is more comfortable communicating with those around her. She will probably be more opinionated and have her unique interests and hobbies. Connecting with your inner child at this stage of your journey is essential, particularly because this is the first stage where you likely have concrete memories.

Begin this visualization exercise by sitting in a comfortable space. Close your eyes and start practicing your breathing techniques, inhaling and exhaling rhythmically. Let the world around you slowly melt away. With every exhale, release the image of the space you are in. Notice how it gently melts away around you, slowly turning to darkness before a soft, warm yellow light starts to glow. Feel the comforting heat radiating from this life and watch how the light and your visualization grow with every inhale. Continue focusing on your breathing and the warmth spreading through your body until you have built up a scene around you for this visualization.

Picture your inner child at around five years old, just towards the end of her preschool days. She is sitting at a table, perhaps in your childhood kitchen or living room, and is messily drawing in a coloring book. Though she cannot help but draw outside the lines, her face is pleased and satisfied with her work. However, when she looks around, there is no one there to appreciate her art. Glumly, she turns back to the page and picks up a new color crayon. She continues to color, perhaps less enthusiastic this time.

Approach her slowly as the scene begins to come into more focus. As gently as you can to avoid frightening her, take a seat next to where she is drawing. Allow yourself to sit with her for a few moments while she colors, and notice the page that she is coloring. As a side note, one memento you might want to consider for this visualization is a coloring book from your childhood or your children, if applicable.

In a soft voice, say hello to your inner child. How she responds will not be the same for everyone, so if she does not speak to you, do not worry. Trust takes time to build, and you must let her move at her own pace. Despite how young she is, she is already craving the nurturing love and care of a mother and has already been let down by your mother. Suddenly receiving this attention from you is welcome, but still might make her wary.

Continue speaking to your inner child, regardless of whether or not she replies. Keep your voice low, gentle, and warm. *I like your picture. Is that your favorite animal? I love the colors you chose. You could be an artist with your talent.*

Allow her to continue drawing, interjecting now and then to remind her of your comforting presence. Once she is finished drawing, visualize her turning the page to show you her creation. Congratulate her for her work and tell her that you would love to see more of her art in the future if she is comfortable with that. Show her that you are genuine in your desire to care for and nurture her and that you will support her passions no matter what.

Before exiting this visualization, say some parting words to your inner child. *Thank you for letting me visit and see your art. I hope you will share more of it with me in the future. I love you. I am here for you whenever you need me.*

Now, walk out of the door of your childhood home and back into the present moment. Take a few deep breaths and slowly open your eyes. Sit still for a moment, taking in everything around you. If you are working with a memento, then shift your attention to the object at hand. Study everything about it. How does it look, feel, and sound? What emotions does it evoke in you? How does your inner child relate to this object? Journal your thoughts if you feel that this would help.

Visualization for Stage Five: Junior School Age

This stage of childhood begins at the age of five or six and lasts until the age of 11, when a child typically begins secondary school. At this stage, you likely have clear memories of your childhood and interactions with your covert, narcissistic mother. Additionally, this stage is often a turning point in a child's academic development, as their studies begin to have a greater impact on their daily life and future.

Furthermore, stage five is when children begin learning how to build and enforce stricter boundaries with the surrounding people. During this time, a child will also learn how to recognize and correct their mistakes and will develop more advanced skills in areas such as writing, drawing, and concentration.

The ability to develop and enforce boundaries naturally involves some level of independence on the child's behalf. However, daughters of narcissistic mothers are not granted the opportunity to develop healthy independence from their mothers. As a result of this, visualization five will focus on developing independence for your inner child and helping her set boundaries for how she wants to be treated.

Begin this visualization in the same way you have in the previous exercises. Sitting in a comfortable space where you will not be interrupted, close your eyes and begin breathing in deeply, allowing the room around you to melt away with each inhale. Though you are not physically near anyone, your inner child is next to you, ready to begin. Feel her presence and become comfortable existing in the same space as her.

As you inhale, build a scene in your mind. Picture your child around the age of seven or eight. At this stage, she is craving some form of independence and wants to start doing things on her own without the influence of anyone around her. Instead of clinging to her, be there to nurture her and be ready to lend a helping hand whenever she needs your guidance. Imagine that you and she are in your childhood home, in the entryway where you keep all of your shoes. She is sitting on the floor, knee bent and nearly touching her face. Her shoulders are crouched, her body leaning in on itself.

Picture her expression, determined and resilient. Do not speak to her yet–instead, allow the scene to play out in front of you, watching as she takes the lead in controlling her actions. She has a shoe on her right foot and is doing her best to tie it. She has not yet been taught how to do this on her own, but she wants to learn, to develop some sense of independence, even in something as small as this task. Watch as she pulls on her shoelaces, allowing her to continue trying even if she falters.

At this point, your inner child may have recognized your presence. If she has, allow her to acknowledge you on her own time, and only give her advice if she asks this of you. Instead of giving advice, offer her words of encouragement. *You can do this. You're doing amazing. I am so proud of you.* Let her know that she is loved and cared for and that, while you respect her independence, you will always be there if she needs you.

While learning to tie your shoelaces may seem like a small, insignificant step in life, this action shows a sign of developing independence for a child. The pride that your inner child feels at this moment is something to be celebrated, not ignored. No matter how big or small the action is, tell your inner child that you will always be there to cheer her on along her journey.

Study your inner child, noticing how she slowly switches her strategy as she becomes more familiar with the process. Stay with her until she has successfully tied her shoes, and watch as she stands up, her shoulders held high with pride and the joy from her accomplishment evident on her face. At this time, tell her again that you are proud of her. *I am always here to help you when you need me, but I am proud you are growing and learning every step of the way. Thank you for letting me be here to witness this.*

Your inner child may choose to speak with you at this time; if so, allow her to say what is on her mind, encouraging her to express her unfiltered thoughts, whether these are positive or negative. Converse with her if she seems receptive to a discussion. If she does not speak, this is okay, too—she knows that you are there and recognizes your presence as something comforting and nurturing.

As you prepare to leave this visualization, leave your inner child with a gentle goodbye. You may ask for permission to hug her, hold her hand, or perform other signs of love and comfort. Shift your attention back to your breathing, keeping the same rhythm as you have been. With each exhale, allow the visualization to fade around you, but still notice your inner child's presence deep inside you. As you inhale, bring yourself back to the present moment. If you are using a memento for this visualization, slowly open your eyes and take the object in. Hold it close to your chest and feel its power radiating through you, tying you closer to your inner child.

Give your inner child one last word of thanks and allow your breathing to return to its natural pattern. Look at the room around you and ground yourself back in the present. You may choose to list objects or colors that you see in the room or ground yourself by touching things around you. Feel free to journal any thoughts you have after this visualization and do your best to capture the scene in detail, especially if you were able to communicate with your inner child.

Visualization for Stage Six: Secondary School Age

The penultimate stage of childhood lasts from the ages of 11 to 14, right before the child enters high school. Because this is an important and stressful time for many children, you must communicate with your inner child and guide her through this process. Therefore, this visualization will focus on your inner child as she is preparing to start high school.

Sitting in a comfortable, isolated area, close your eyes and begin breathing rhythmically. As you breathe, start building up a scene in your mind. Because this time period leads up to high school, imagine that you are in an auditorium, with eager parents taking up all the seats and students lining up by the stage in their graduation caps and gowns. In this line, notice your inner child around the age of 13. She is standing just in the middle of the line, looking around nervously at all the people watching her and her classmates.

Notice how your inner child catches your eye, and give her an encouraging smile and a thumbs up if you would like. A simple gesture of reassurance goes a long way in moments like these, and your inner child deserves to be celebrated for her many accomplishments thus far. Watch as the students begin taking to the stage, going one by one as their names are announced. For each student whose name is called, there are some light cheers and applause from the audience of family members. All the students shake the principal's hand as they are given a certificate showing their achievement.

Soon, it is your inner child's turn. As she makes her way up to the stage, her legs trembling ever so slightly, cheer for her. Make sure that she can hear you clearly, and continue clapping and cheering as she shakes hands and accepts the certificate. When she looks in your direction, give her a bright, brilliant smile. Watch how her face lights up as she smiles back at you, the pride that comes through in her expression.

Moments like these are rare–or nonexistent–in a scapegoat daughter's childhood. While you did not receive the loving support and pride from your mother that you needed at this age, that does not mean that you cannot give love back to your inner child and be there for the moments your mother missed. Remember that you are taking on the role of mother in many ways, that you are the only one who can truly nurture, care for, and love your inner child.

As she exits the stage, notice your inner child making her way towards you, happiness still etched on her face. Because your inner child is older now, communication between the two of you will come easier, especially if you have worked to openly communicate with her during other stages of her childhood. Open your arms to her and notice how comforting it is for her to wrap her arms around you and hug you closely.

As you hold her, begin to speak. Again, reaffirm how proud you are of her and her accomplishments. *I am so proud of you. This is a huge step towards your future. I knew you were strong enough to do this, but I still couldn't be more proud. I am so excited to see you as you embark on this new journey. I love you.*

Your inner child may choose to reply to you at this stage. Listen to what she has to say, placing your entire focus on her and the words she uses to express her emotions. Allow her to speak her mind, and when she is finished, offer her your hand. When she takes your hand, begin walking side by side, hands held as you make your way into her future, into the vast opportunities she has at her disposal. Continue walking until you leave the auditorium, go outside, and feel the fresh air on your skin.

When you notice the air hit you, inhale deeply and steadily. Notice how the cool air courses through your lungs and lights up your body. Turn towards your inner child and thank her for letting you be there to celebrate this moment. Now, begin coming back into the present moment. Keep inhaling and exhaling steadily, imagining how it would feel to breathe in the fresh air in your visualization. As a side note, you may consider keeping a window open during this visualization if you can and if it does not distract you from your goal.

Breathe in and out until you feel fully present. Slowly open your eyes, taking in everything around you. A possible memento you might use for this exercise is a graduation certificate or diploma from this stage of your childhood. If you have this on hand, study the paper and imagine the look on your inner child's face as she accepted it, recalling how happy you were to see her thriving. You will witness many moments like this with your inner child as you continue down the path of healing.

Visualization for Stage Seven: High School Age

The final stage of childhood covers the typical high school years, most often the ages of 15 to 18. Your inner child is more independent now, and she is looking ahead to her future. Recall the emotions that you went through at this stage of your childhood. Were you nervous, excited, joyful, or all of the above? What words would you use to describe this period?

Once you have identified some of the emotions you felt at this stage of your life, get into a comfortable position and close your eyes. Inhale and exhale slowly but steadily, feeling how each breath lights up your body, giving you life. Again, build the scene of your visualization around you as you inhale, and let go of your present space as you exhale.

In this visualization, imagine your inner child at the age of 17. She is on the cusp of graduating, with only a few months left until her birthday and the end of her high school career. As the daughter of a narcissistic mother, this time in your life might have been challenging. It is not uncommon that a covert narcissist mother gets upset at your choices during this time, especially if you choose to attend a university far from your hometown. She may use various tactics to guilt and manipulate you into staying closer to her or staying at your home with her. Because of this, you want to build a visualization that corrects the past to provide your inner child with the support your mother neglected to offer you.

This visualization will be somewhat similar to the scene presented in the introduction, but with a far more positive outcome. Imagine that you are sitting at home, and your inner child enters through the door. There is excitement and glee on her face, and you can tell that she has received some pleasing news. She skips over to you, barely holding back what she is about to say.

Offer your inner child a smile that is as radiant as her own. Ideally, you will be able to comfortably communicate with your inner child at this stage and have an open discussion with her. Imagine your inner child coming over to sit beside you, excitedly saying: *Guess what?*

Envision your inner child pulling a letter out of her bag and sliding it over to you. Gently pick the letter up, unfolding it carefully as though it is a fragile thing. Notice the joy in your inner child's face and the anticipation in the air as you begin reading the letter. It is a letter of acceptance to her dream college, the one that she has been talking about for years. Over time, she has expressed to you worries that she will not be accepted, but you have stood by her side and encouraged her every step of the way.

After you read the letter, embrace your inner child. Hold her in your arms and tell her how proud you are of her, that you have always believed in her and knew that she could do this. *You can do anything you set your mind to. I am so proud of you. I can't wait to see how you thrive in the future.*

Because you are taking on the role of mother for your inner child, you should go the extra mile to celebrate her successes. You are her biggest cheerleader, and while you have encouraged her to develop independence over the years, you have always remained on the sidelines in case she needs you. You can continue doing this even into her adulthood. While this event marks the end of the stages of childhood, she is still your child and will always need your nurturing love and support.

Continue embracing your inner child, responding to anything that she says as you hold her. She has grown so much since the first visualization, but she is still the strong, resilient fighter that she was at the start. You have watched her grow, staying by her side whenever things got tough and celebrating all of her accomplishments. She can go into her adulthood now, knowing that she will have your unyielding support no matter what path she takes. Regardless of what happens next, she knows that she will have her mother's love.

Before you leave this meditation, kiss your inner child on her forehead. Leave her with loving words as you depart: *I love you so much. Thank you for letting me be a part of your childhood and your life. I will always be here to support and love you. Your strength and independence inspire me, and you will always be my priority in life. Whenever you need nurturing, I am here. Whenever something goes wrong, I will help you get through it. Whether you are celebrating your achievements or grieving your mistakes, I will be by your side, defending you the whole time. Thank you for this opportunity. I love you.*

Stay with your inner child as long as you would like, speaking nurturing words or simply remaining in an embrace with her. When you are ready to disengage from the scene, shift your attention back to your breathing. As your breathing returns to its natural rhythm, slowly open your eyes and take in everything around you. Feel the joy in your body, the happiness at how much your inner child has accomplished and will accomplish in the future. Allow the positive feelings to radiate through your body, filling you with warmth and hope. There are so many amazing things to come in the future for both you and your inner child. As long as you have each other, you can take on anything the world throws your way.

···•·•••···

After you go through these visualizations, you may want to take time to ponder what you witnessed and write down anything that surprised you. Below are some questions to ask yourself after you complete any of these visualizations. If you would like to answer after each visualization, then you can write down some of your responses in your journal. You may also answer these questions after you have completed all the visualizations.

Which stage of childhood did you visualize?

✎

Was the visualization(s) you completed similar to how it was described here? What differed, if anything?

✎

Did you speak with your inner child or communicate with her nonverbally? If yes, describe what happened below.

🖎

What emotions did you feel when you saw your inner child in this visualization(s)?

🖎

Which mementos did you use, if any? Why did you select this memento?

🖎

What did you learn about your inner child that you had not before?

🖎

Was there anything you wanted to say to your inner child that you did not get the chance to?

🖎

Do you feel closer to your inner child now than you did before the visualization?

🖎

What three things are you taking away from this visualization(s)? For instance, you may choose to list emotions, lessons your inner child taught you, new perspectives you have, etc. 🖎

· · · · •· • • · · ·

Healing your inner child wounds will inevitably require you to move through your past, even further back than you can clearly remember. Because you are becoming a mother to your inner child, you want to be with her for every step of her journey, as though you are truly raising a child–because, in many ways, you are. As you watch your inner child grow and practice visualizations for the seven stages of childhood, you can give your inner child the nurturing love she craves and which both of you need. The following chapter will go through practices to essentially "rewrite" your past once you understand your inner child's progress during the stages of childhood.

Chapter Seven

Reshaping Your Childhood

As discussed in the previous chapter, healing from inner child wounds requires you to picture your child at every stage of her life, witnessing her accomplishments and cheering her on no matter what happens. Doing so is an act of motherly love towards your inner child, as you give her the nurturing that you craved at her age. Because you and your inner child are the same, it is important to reshape her childhood and envision your childhood memories more healthily.

Below, you will find an exercise that presents you with questions about specific childhood memories. First, you will be encouraged to describe these events in detail, as much as you are comfortable with. Following this, you will be given space to rework the memories that you described. Essentially, you will put yourself in the position of your inner child's mother.

As you reimagine these moments, write about the experience once again from the perspective of how you would have liked that situation to play out. I have begun by offering an example of this method to act as a guideline for the journaling questions within this exercise below.

Describe a memory from your childhood when you presented your mother with good news that she brushed aside. Explain how her dismissal of your positive emotions made you feel and any harmful messages you internalized from this moment. Use as much detail as possible.

✎ *When I was 14 and just beginning high school, I remember coming home one day to my mother. She knew I had been struggling in my first high school math class, and that math was my lowest grade. Because I had already internalized the idea that I had to be perfect, struggling so much at school and witnessing my mother's disappointment took a toll on my mental health. One day, I got a 100% grade on my math exam after studying hard for days. When I arrived back, I showed my mom the exam, feeling happy and hopeful about the class. However, my mother merely told me "Good job. Let's see if you can keep that up. After all, it might just be a fluke." She returned to whatever she was doing and didn't mention the test again. I felt devalued, ashamed, and untalented, and after this event, I began telling her less and less about my accomplishments.*

Now, rework this memory. Imagine your inner child presenting you with the same good news. How would you have liked your mother to respond to this situation? What did you need from your mother that you did not get? How can you give this to your child as you reimagine this scenario? How does your positive reaction make your inner child feel? Use as much detail as possible.

✎ *In this memory, my inner child comes home to me and tells me that she has good news. She has been struggling in math, and while I reassured her and helped her study, she was still worried about an upcoming exam. However, she came to me ecstatic and showed me her 100% grade. I was so proud of her and her hard work. I hugged her, holding her tightly and telling her how proud I was and that I knew she could do amazing. I also told her that whenever she needed my help, I would aid her in studying for future exams. Because of her achievement, I took her out to dinner that night at a restaurant of her choosing.*

Exercise to Rework Childhood Experiences

Below, you will be asked questions of a similar style. Answer honestly, using the above example as a guide. Take your time and come back to any questions that feel too overwhelming.

1. Recall a time in your childhood when you broke something or made a mistake. Describe how your mother responded when she found out. Did she say anything in particular? How did her reaction make you feel? What did you take away from this experience, and how did it change how you acted around your mother? Use as much detail as possible.

2. Imagine the same scenario, placing yourself in the position of your mother and your inner child as your daughter. She makes the same m. Imagine the same scenario, placing yourself in the position of your mother and your inner child as your daughter. She makes the same mistake and comes to you to apologize. How do you respond to let her know that her apology is accepted and that you are not angry with her? How do you make her feel more comfortable coming to you when things go wrong? What do you want her to know by the end of this conversation? Use as much detail as possible.

3. Imagine yourself as a child who has just gotten her first period. You go to your mother to tell her and ask for help in learning what steps to take next. However, your mother does not offer you help when you tell her that you got your period. You do not want to ask for her help because she will say she is too busy. All of your friends who have gotten their period turned to their mothers for advice and guidance. How do you feel, knowing

that your mother did not give you that attention? What did you internalize through this experience? How did your relationship with your mother change? Use as much detail as possible.

✎

4. Imagine the same scenario. Your inner child comes to you and tells you that she has gotten her first period. She seems nervous because of this massive change in her life. How do you help her navigate the situation? Do you teach her how to take care of herself? How do you let her know that you are there to help her and that she can come to you with any questions? How do you grow closer to her through this experience? Use as much detail as possible.

✎

5. Imagine a time in your childhood when you struggled to regulate your emotions. For instance, picture a time when you were playing with your sibling or a friend. Your sibling or friend has a toy that you want, and you were supposed to have your turn ten minutes ago. When you ask them for the toy, they refuse to give it to you. You try to grab it out of their hand, but they don't let go, and you begin to cry and yell. You do not know how to control your emotions in this situation, and your mother scolds you later for your response. How is this reaction a result of your mother's lack of nurturing and communication? Use as much detail as possible.

✎

6. Picture the same scenario. Your inner child gets into an argument with a sibling or friend, which ends in a tantrum. What do you say to her after removing yourself from the situation? How can you kindly and gently explain why her behavior was not appropriate? How could you help her improve her communication skills so that she can verbally say what she is feeling and healthily express her frustrations? Use as much detail as possible.

7. Think of something significant you hid from your mother in the later stages of childhood. Describe why you hid this from her and what reaction you think she may have had if you told her. For instance, if something bad happened to you or someone in your life, you got into trouble for something, or you performed poorly at school/sports. How do you think she would have responded if you told her? How would this impact your relationship or make you feel ashamed? Use as much detail as possible.

8. Imagine your inner child anxious over telling you a secret. Something significant has happened to her, but she struggles to find the words to tell you. However, because you have always encouraged communication with her, she musters up the courage to admit to what happened. How do you respond? If she made a mistake, how do you gently teach her about this mistake? How do you ensure that she does not feel ashamed, and that she knows you

are not disappointed in her? What do you say in response, and how do you communicate nonverbally? Use as much detail as possible.

✎

9. Now, think of a time in your childhood when you not only omitted the truth from your mother, but outright lied to her. Lying in one form or another is something that most children do at some stage in their childhood due to external stressors or preconceived fears about their parents' reactions. In this scenario, you are lying to your mother because you are afraid that, if you tell the truth, she will be angry and disappointed with you. Even though you feel guilty about the lie, you do not admit that you have been dishonest. Why do you think you would rather maintain the lie instead of telling your mother the truth? How do you think she would react if you admitted to your lie? How often do you lie to your mother in general? Use as much detail as possible.

✎

10. Think of a scenario where your inner child is hiding something from you. You might notice that something is wrong, but she seems anxious and unsure. She knows she can tell you if she has done something, but is still nervous about approaching you. Despite this, she feels guilty for telling you a false story and decides that owning up to her lie is better than maintaining something untrue. She comes to you and tells you that she lied, apologizing and expressing guilt. How do you tell her that, while she did not need to lie, you are grateful that she opened up and told you the

truth eventually? How do you reassure her that you will not judge her on her truth, no matter what happens? How do you teach her to be more honest in the future whenever she needs something from you? Is there a way you might have approached your inner child when you felt she was acting strange? Use as much detail as possible.

Post-Rewrite Meditation

The above exercise is often challenging because it requires you to dive deep into painful memories. When we think of how we wish our mother treated us, feelings of sadness, resentment, and frustration commonly arise. Even if you know how to better regulate these emotions, you must have ways to calm yourself after this exercise. A brief post-exercise meditation is essential for this and will help you recognize the core of the previous exercise: understanding precisely what your inner child needs from you.

Below is a meditation that you can turn to at any stage during the above exercise or whenever you find yourself overwhelmed after reflecting on childhood memories. This meditation, provided by Barrie Davenport (2022), will help you let go of the negative emotions you associate with childhood memories, making it possible for you to move forward and create new, positive experiences with your inner child.

1. Sit in a quiet, calming, and comfortable space where you can be alone and analyze your surroundings. Look around the room, noticing anything that feels familiar to you or anything that seems different. Whatever you notice, accept this environment.

2. Once your body has relaxed into a comfortable position, allow your eyes to slowly close as you begin to look inwards. Inhale through your nose and exhale through your mouth steadily, counting if you feel that it would be helpful. Seek out your inner child until you feel her presence.

3. Now, feel your mind open as you accept this memory into your headspace. Examine whatever thoughts and feelings you notice at this moment, not judging them but simply observing.

4. As you think of this memory, begin visualizing a new space. You can picture your mind as a comfortable, tidy room. The walls may be lined with shelves or neatly decorated with paintings and photographs. Each book, image, or artwork on the wall contains one of your memories. You may also choose to picture your mind as a storage closet, neatly organized with all of your childhood memories.

5.   Take in all of the details around you as you settle into this new environment. Accept the memories that you find in this space, good or bad, as a part of you. Denying the past is not healthy, but getting caught up in memories will deter you from healing with your inner child.

6.   Go through the memories you find in the room. Looking at each of them one by one, accept the situation and what you experienced as a child. Notice which memories call out to you the most, and which ones you are hesitant to touch. Are there specific boxes of memories that you avoid? Are there pictures that you want to turn away? What speaks to you most?

7.   Once you have gone through your memories, embrace the possibility of change. Your inner child does not have to follow in your footsteps, and you have the chance to create new, wonderful memories with her by your side. Feel the hope for a change of course through your body, illuminating all the possibilities ahead of you.

8.   Begin to leave this space. Imagine that there is a door in the room, and behind the door is the space that your physical body is sitting in. With one last look at the memories to acknowledge their validity, turn and exit through the door.

9.   Slowly open your eyes, keeping your breath steady. Take in the space around you, and once again, notice anything that stands

out to you. Ground yourself in the present moment through touch, sound, or sight.

10.   Thank your inner child for going on this journey with you, and move forward knowing that you can create new, loving memories for her.

· · · ·•·•·•· · ·

While I worked on healing my inner child, I found that one of the most troubling aspects I ran into was feelings of sadness and remorse. I wanted to give my inner child everything that I never had from my mother, but doing so meant that I would have to reflect on painful memories and experiences that I thought I had moved past.

I consider my inner child to be my daughter, not merely a part of me, but her individual as well. Going through these painful memories with her was gut-wrenching at times, and enlightening at others. However, no matter how challenging a memory was, I took comfort in knowing that I could reshape this memory and create new, loving memories by nurturing my inner child. It is possible to let go and accept without forcing yourself to forget your experiences. As you navigate inner child healing exercises, remember that there is always room for change and that, through

nurturing your inner child, you simultaneously take care of yourself.

Chapter Eight

Breaking Unhealthy Childhood Patterns

W HILE YOU HAVE DEVELOPED more maturity as an adult, there are unseen patterns in your life that are rooted in your childhood trauma. Your inner child clings on to unhealthy habits and patterns, which you still partake in as an adult. Therefore, a significant part of inner child healing is learning how to recognize and break your unhealthy childhood patterns. By doing this, you will unmask your subconscious thoughts and emotions and challenge your toxic belief system.

Differentiating Between Child and Adult Self

Before you can understand how you unconsciously adhere to unhealthy childhood patterns and beliefs, you need to understand the differences and similarities between your child and adult self. Though you are an adult, your inner child still expresses herself in many ways. Differentiating between these two parts of you will allow you to see how you have changed over time, and how you have stayed the same.

To recognize the key differences between yourself and your inner child, you will go through a brief exercise inspired by Bethany Webster (n.d.). This exercise will take you through the two primary steps of breaking unhealthy childhood patterns: validating and differentiating. Each step will be explained with an example. After these two stages, you will be guided through the process of sharing a positive vision with your inner child to build a safe, nurturing environment. To conclude the exercise, you will be asked to respond to a few short questions to process your experience.

Step One: Validate

One of the reasons your inner child hides herself is because her emotions have never been validated in the past. Because of the pain that results from revisiting childhood memories, you have, perhaps unconsciously, pushed your inner child away and ignored her emotions. Along with this is the fact that your inner child is still operating with your childhood mindset, where you believed that your mother did not value your emotions, opinions, and beliefs. As a result, one of the first things you need to do whenever you communicate with your inner child is to validate what she feels at that moment.

Begin by showing your inner child genuine empathy and care. Reassure her that her emotions are valid and that her thoughts and feelings matter. Tell her that her feelings are normal and that she should not feel bad for how she feels due to her mother's treatment and neglect. Take your time going through what she feels and validating her emotions. Even if this step brings up some unpleasant memories, do your best to power through and connect with your inner child, giving her a voice to speak up in a way she never has before.

Think back to your past and identify a time when your mother devalued your emotions. Recall how it felt when your mother willfully ignored your needs and criticized you for your natural emotions. This pain is your inner child's pain, and healing that pain requires you to go back to the initial moment and reframe the situation.

As you process your feelings about specific childhood events, speak to your inner child and yourself: *It is not your fault. What happened to us is in no way a reflection of who we are as a person. What we feel as a result of the abuse we experienced is natural, normal, and valid. Do not feel guilty for expressing how you feel or any unpleasant emotions you experience. Just because my mother did not validate us does not mean that I cannot validate you now. We can digest the past and start to let go of this pain through validation.*

Take a deep breath and allow the pain to be released when you exhale. When you connect your inner child's repressed emotions to specific occurrences in your childhood, you are building a path to acknowledgment and healing with your inner child.

You can continue speaking to your inner child if she is open to further communication. Continue validating her when she doubts herself and pay attention to how she feels as you start to recall different childhood memories. Always give her the reminder she needs: *what you feel is a natural result of your experiences. I will never judge you for your emotions, and I will never let you be alone again. You can tell me anything without fear of reprimanding. I will always validate what you are feeling and help guide you towards a healthier, healed mindset. I am sorry for the suffering you have experienced, but I am here to ensure that it will never happen again as it did in our childhood.*

Step Two: Differentiate

Following the initial validation step, start to differentiate between yourself and your inner child. You have acknowledged and validated your experiences, but it is essential to realize that these memories are nothing more than that: experiences, memories that should not dictate your adult life. In this step, you want to identify every way that your present life differs from the past and all of the ways that your inner child has changed.

Tell your inner child: *Now differs from the past. You don't have to be afraid to express how you feel anymore—we are not in the same place we used to be. The pain you feel is not your fault and never has been. No matter what happens, you are good, whole, and worthy of all the care and nurturing I offer.*

Keep a loving, gentle tone in your voice as you communicate with your inner child. You will want to use concrete examples during this step of the process and select memories or emotions that are vivid in your mind and the mind of your inner child. The more detailed your examples are about how life has changed, the better. By offering comprehensive examples, your inner child will truly be able to differentiate between the past and the present, allowing her to feel safer existing now. This exercise will remind your inner child that she is safe and protected now and that the past cannot hurt her.

Tell your inner child: *You will never be alone again. You never have to be afraid to show who you really are again. The environment we grew up in differs from the safe space we have created now. You will never be unprotected or unsupported ever again. I am here to take care of you, love you, and nurture you in every step of your journey. Whenever you need me to comfort you, I will always be by your side. You are safe here with me.*

Step Three: Sharing a Positive Vision

The final step of this exercise allows you to connect with your inner child by sharing an inspiring and comforting vision of the road ahead. Your inner child knows things can differ from the way they were in the past and that it is possible to move forward and heal. Now, you must show her how you will accomplish this together.

Your shared positive vision can be as brief or detailed as you and your inner child are comfortable with. The goal of this step is to create a vision where your inner child feels safe, nurtured, and liberated. As you continue practicing this exercise over time, you may choose to have the vision become more detailed and specific to your situation.

For instance, sharing a positive vision with your inner child may involve making plans for what you and she can do after this exercise. You may choose to say to your inner child: *We are constantly healing and moving forward. The progress you have made is inspiring, and we will continue to accept joy and fun in our life. Let's go outside and take a walk. We can go to the park or simply walk around in nature and enjoy the sunshine and fresh air.*

Then follow through on your promise to your inner child. If you chose to go outside and take a walk around your neighborhood, for example, you can stand by your inner child's side and take note of everything you see. Watch with her as you take in the birds chirping and flying around, the feeling of warm sun on your face and a cool breeze against your skin, or the sound of kids playing on a playground nearby. Allow the beauty of this experience to wash over you as nature embraces your inner child. Through this, you will continue healing from your inner child's wounds by recognizing the beautiful, endless possibilities stretching out ahead of you.

··•·•·•·•··

Following this exercise, journal your thoughts using the questions below as prompts to describe your experience.

1.   What emotion or emotions did you validate during this exercise? Why do you think your inner child hid these emotions from you specifically?

✎

2. Can you connect the emotions discovered in step one of this exercise with specific instances in your childhood?

✎

3.   How are things different now? Do you feel like your inner child is more comfortable sharing her emotions with you now? Why or why not? ✎

4. Do you feel closer to your inner child? During this exercise, did you take on a "motherly" role?

✎

5. What are some additional positive visions you can share with your inner child when practicing this exercise in the future?

✎

· · · ● · ● · · · ·

To strengthen the effectiveness of the above exercise, you will want to specifically determine how your current attitude and behavioral patterns reflect the patterns you exhibited in childhood. Often, daughters of narcissistic mothers unconsciously treat their inner child as a scapegoat, adopting similar relationship patterns to their mothers. To truly heal your inner child, you must recognize how you have failed her in some ways and how you can correct your belief system to ensure that you will never harm her again.

Below, you will find questions encouraging you to dissect your current attitudes and patterns and if they are like how you behaved in childhood. This exercise will help you better understand what your inner child needs from you regarding behavior and actions.

When you recognize these harmful patterns, you can begin embracing positive patterns in your life.

As an adult, do you feel you need to earn the love of others? How do you get approval from those around you?

✎

When something bad happens, what do you say to yourself? For instance, are you more inclined to tell yourself "I don't deserve to be treated like this," or to say "This is all my fault, and I deserve all the bad things that happen to me"?

✎

What are some of your biggest social fears? For example, when you are out in public, do you fear being humiliated, ignored, devalued, or otherwise harmed? Do you isolate yourself frequently?

✎

Do you express your needs to other people and enforce boundaries for how you should be treated? If you do not, what is holding you back?

✎

Do you often let other people decide for you? Do you not trust yourself to make the right choices for serious life matters?

✎

Do you fear abandonment and go out of your way to ensure that the people close to you do not leave you? When relationships have ended in the past, how did you react?

✎

When something is not right in one of your relationships, do you address the issue or ignore it? How do you approach conflict in your personal relationships?

✎

As an adult, have you entered a relationship where you knew you were being treated poorly but stayed to gain mastery over the situation?

✎

How do you speak to yourself? Is your self-talk positive or negative?

✎

Do you avoid opportunities because you are afraid of failing or convince yourself prematurely that you will not be successful?

✎

As an adult, have you ever–intentionally or unintentionally–changed yourself and your personality to gain the respect and love of others?

✎

Do you struggle to tell other people the full truth because you are afraid of making them upset?

✎

Do you feel like there is a part of you missing? Is there an absence of self-love or purpose in your life?

✎

When looking at your responses to previous questions, do you notice similarities between yourself and a member of your family that were prominent in your childhood?

✎

After documenting your thoughts, you will want to take time and seriously consider how your responses are like how you would have responded in childhood. Are your responses indicative of a deeply rooted sense of shame? Do you see more similarities between your adult and child selves than differences? Take time to reflect on how you have emulated your mother's behavior and directed your sadness and anger toward your inner child.

· · • • • • • • · ·

Following the above exercise, I often like to bring myself back to the present moment by practicing meditation aimed at breaking unhealthy patterns. Once I have recognized the harmful childhood patterns impacting my adulthood, I can strengthen my resolve to change by concluding with a calming, grounding meditation, such as the two provided below. While you do not have to wait to use these meditations until after you have completed the exercise, I find that it is most effective for me if completed after clearly identifying toxic childhood patterns.

Meditation One: Breaking Unhealthy Childhood Patterns

Identifying and breaking unhealthy patterns is possible when you have a greater awareness of yourself, your inner child, and the world at large. While you may use typical mindfulness meditation to foster this awareness, there are other methods that you may not have practiced which will provide you with new insight into your wounded inner child. One of these practices is Vipassana meditation, often referred to simply as "insight" meditation.

Using the Vipassana method will encourage you to go through your unhealthy childhood patterns and understand them without judgment. Your inner child needs to find a place where she can express her pain and struggles without fear of reprimanding or shaming you, the mother figure.

The following steps will guide you through a typical Vipassana meditation session as described by mindfulness and meditation teacher Paul Harrison (2014). Throughout this meditation, I will encourage you to find connections with your inner child and specific memories that have contributed to your unhealthy childhood patterns.

1.   Begin this meditation by sitting in a relaxing space where you will be free of external distractions. You may choose to sit in a chair during this exercise, but make sure you are maintaining a good posture and remain in a comfortable position.

2.   Allow your eyes to close as the room disappears around you. Notice your inner child and her presence by your side. If you cannot feel her next to you, remind yourself that she is still there, deep inside of you, witnessing everything you undergo.

3.   Take a deep breath in, feeling how the air expands your chest and pulling it down into your stomach. Notice how your abdomen feels and focus on this area of your body. While your breathing should be deep, it should also be relaxed and comfortable.

4.   Continue breathing, focusing on the sensation of your breath as it enters your body through your nose and exits through your mouth. If you would like, you can visualize the path that the air takes as it makes its way through your body, filling you with energy and life.

5.   As you focus on your breathing and the gentle rise and fall of your abdomen, raise your awareness about the entire breathing process. Notice everything that you can about your breathing as you take about 25 mindful breaths.

6.   Breathe in and out with your body and mind, noticing how both are crucial to practice your breathing. Your body will lead while your mind follows.

7.   Allow your mind to rest as you focus all your attention on your breathing. It is essential to avoid looking at breathing as a three-step process during this exercise. Instead of the typical process of inhaling, pausing, and exhaling, you should see your breath as one smooth movement.

8.   There are times in any meditation when you might lose focus on your breathing. In Vipassana meditation, these distractions can be turned into a learning moment and offer you insight into your inner child's belief system. Be gentle and compassionate with yourself and your inner child during this meditation, even if you feel like you are not getting it "right" the first time. When you notice that your mind has begun to wander, identify what it is you are thinking about. Perhaps a specific memory or emotion comes to mind that you typically avoid dealing with. Instead of pushing it to the side, notice the feeling and place a label on it. For instance, name any emotion you feel, stating out loud "sadness," "guilt," "grief," etc.

9. Once you have labeled this emotion, gently shift your attention back to your breathing, focusing on how the breath sounds, tastes, and feels as it fills your abdomen. Describe the movement of your breath quietly to yourself to maintain focus.

10. You might run into issues if you are distracted by any external factors. For instance, if you hear the sound of birds outside or someone loudly walking around upstairs, your mind will naturally be taken away from the meditation. It is impossible to predict or prevent this from happening, but you can implement the distraction into your meditation. When you hear a noise, mindfully observe, accept, and again label the distraction as "sound." Doing this helps your mind process external stimuli before shifting your focus back to your breath.

11. You can also label any other stimuli that distract you from your meditation. If you feel a sensation in your body, label it. If you notice any glaring thoughts or imaginings, label these as well.

12. If any specific memories of your childhood arise, let the scene play out and try to understand why your inner child is showing you this memory. Once you understand the memory, label it with any word that seems most fitting. You could identify emotions to describe how the memory makes you feel, or choose a word that describes what happened in this memory.

13.   To end your Vipassana meditation, gently open your eyes. As your eyes slowly flutter open, repeat the word "opening" to yourself. Then, state what you intend to do after your initial meditation. As you choose what you will do after, repeat the word "intending" while your mind settles.

14.   Go about the rest of your day from a new, mindful perspective. Label whatever grabs your attention throughout the day, cultivating a new understanding of your everyday life.

This meditation is incredibly valuable for daughters of narcissistic mothers because it encourages radical self-acceptance of your past and your inner child's troubling emotions. When you meditate and truly let your mind go, you allow your inner child to take control and communicate with you. By accepting your inner child's emotions, behaviors, and experiences, you gain insight into what your inner child needs from you and how you can help her overcome toxic patterns.

Meditation Two: Breaking Negative Self-Talk Patterns

Another meditation that helps break harmful childhood patterns is a meditation aimed at breaking negative self-talk patterns specifically. Patterns typically develop without you realizing it and eventually become muscle memory. If you grew up being told negative things about yourself by your mother, you inevitably began repeating these negative things to yourself in private.

Given your mother's treatment, you may find that you still instantly jump to negative self-talk when anything goes wrong. Getting rid of these thoughts can feel impossible for anyone, especially because society frequently normalizes sarcastic self-hate and negative self-talk. Over time, these patterns can become detrimental to your health and well-being and that of your inner child.

Below is a step-by-step guide to meditation (Winston, 2018) that will help you break negative self-talk and overcome the pattern of putting yourself down. Try to practice this meditation regularly, as overcoming obsessive negative thoughts takes time, patience, and effort.

1.   Begin by finding a comfortable space where you can sit comfortably while maintaining a good posture. Keep your body upright without making it too rigid and tense. Place your feet on the floor and allow your hands to rest in your lap. Close your eyes or turn your gaze downwards, avoiding any visual distractions.

2.   Start taking notice of your breathing. Meditation always begins with an awareness of one's breath. Begin with a few steady, deep breaths, feeling how your body relaxes more and more with each breath you take. As you focus on your breathing, feel relief in knowing that your problems do not matter right now in this safe space. Leave any worries or concerns behind, for the time being, allowing yourself to relax in your oasis.

3.   If any of your worries or concerns pop into your mind, remind yourself that you do not have to continue pursuing these thoughts right now. Come into the present moment, leaving external issues behind.

4.   Shift attention to your stomach, and feel how your belly expands with each inhale and shrinks with each exhale. If you feel tightness in your stomach or body, allow this sensation to melt away when you release your breath. Relax your hands, and notice any other tense areas in your body. Take note of any body part that you can feel during this time, and release the tension from any area where the muscles feel tight.

5.   Continue breathing, and shift your attention to where you feel your breath the most. Where do you feel the breath most clearly? Perhaps you are drawn to the rise and fall of your chest as you breathe rhythmically. If you are pulling your breath into your stomach, then you may instead notice how your stomach expands and compresses. You might instead pay attention to how the air feels as it hits your nostrils and moves through your body, or what your mouth feels like when you exhale.

6.   After identifying where you feel the breath in your body, shift your attention to sounds. Listen to one sound after the next. Ideally, you will be in a space where sounds are not overwhelming. Take note of the soft whispers of your air conditioning, the

gentle wind outside, the rain pattering against your window, birds chirping–anything that your mind is drawn towards. Listen to the sound of silence when there is nothing else, or the cycle of sounds coming and going as they please.

7.   Find a focus for your meditation, anchoring your attention through noticing breath in different parts of your body or by listening for a specific sound. Choose whatever feels most interesting and natural to you.

8.   Notice your abdomen again, paying close attention to how it rhythmically moves up and down or how your chest expands and contracts. Breath after breath or sound after sound, stick with your focus and shift your attention back to it if your mind begins to wander. Feel the sensations in your body as you zone in on your focus object.

9.   Label your thoughts if your mind continues to wander as you did in the previous meditation. If a specific emotion or memory comes from your inner child, accept these thoughts into your consciousness before labeling them with words like "imagining," "memory," thinking," or "wondering." Then, bring your attention back to the main focus of this meditation.

10.   Because this exercise is aimed at addressing your negative self-talk patterns, allow the labeling process to continue no matter what enters your mind. You may think of something critical that

you frequently tell yourself. If you notice a judging thought, label it with something like "judgment" or "self-criticism." By assigning words to your negative thoughts, you will be able to understand how your negative self-talk arises and where it originates from.

11.   Continue noticing your self-critical thoughts as they arise, accepting the validity of your inner child's emotions while also recognizing that her self-criticism is not indicative of her true character. Use mindfulness to learn to not judge yourself or your emotional reactions. Allow everything to flow through you, and as you identify ways that you frequently criticize yourself, begin accepting self-compassion into your heart.

12.   Maintain a level of genuine, unyielding kindness and love for yourself and your inner child as you do this meditation. While you will have to face negative thoughts, this exercise helps you understand where the false perception of yourself originates from. Remain curious about everything you discover during this exercise. When you let go of judgment for your thoughts, you can realize how unique and special your mind really is.

13.   Begin reflecting on the overall quality of your meditation. Notice how you are feeling physically and mentally as you bring your meditation to a close, and if you feel like you discovered anything new through this session.

14.   Recall the judging thoughts that you had during the meditation. Think of which ones stuck out to you the most, as these are the ones that frequently wound your inner child.

15.   To finish this meditation, you must practice a brief kindness meditation. Pay attention to any positive emotions you have, or take note of any area of your body that feels lighter. If possible, bring into your mind someone or something that you love deeply.

16.   Repeat kind, loving phrases to yourself and your inner child. You can come up with your own phrases or return to some of the affirmations listed in previous chapters. Tell yourself: *You are safe and protected. Be happy and peaceful moving forward. Accept yourself just as you are, releasing self-judgment. You can give and receive kindness, love, nurturing, and compassion. You do not need to change yourself to deserve love from yourself or others–you deserve it simply through your existence.*

17.   If you are comfortable, consider sending out some of your kind phrases to your closest loved ones. Pay attention to how it feels to express these words to others and mean it with your entire being. Imagine that you are also being sent these messages, and accept the loving responses you get from others.

18.   Try to discern if you are prepared to "take" the kindness as your own. Picture the kindness as a warmth moving through your body, bringing you deep comfort. Are you able to take this kind-

ness and keep it to yourself as you are? Can you bring kindness into your life and your inner child's life and maintain this kindness? Repeat to yourself: *May my inner child and I hold on to this kindness and make it our own. May we hold ourselves with compassion and free ourselves from self-judgment? May we be exactly as we are, with no exceptions. May we continue to love ourselves unconditionally?*

19.   When you are ready, slowly open your eyes and come back to the present moment. Take note of your environment, particularly if anything seems different to you.

·········

Over time, your inner child has grown accustomed to the unhealthy patterns that have carried over into your adult life. Because these patterns are second nature to you, breaking them will take time, effort, determination, and above all, communication with your inner child. While challenging, you have the strength to create new, healthy lifestyle patterns that encourage healing for you and your inner child alike. You are stronger together, and as long as you work to identify the scars from your childhood, you can heal your inner child and move into a brighter future.

Chapter Nine

Working Through Your Triggers

A s you go through the core inner child healing exercises, you will inevitably face past trauma that you and your wounded inner child endured at the hands of your mother. No matter how much we would like, addressing traumatic experiences will never be a walk in the park. The reminders of your past trauma may trigger your inner child and reinforce her harmful beliefs: that she is undeserving, unlovable, and a fraud. Experiences like being criticized by another person about your work, a relationship ending, or being rejected by another person naturally bring about difficult emotions for your inner child.

Unfortunately, while you may try to avoid your triggers at all costs, there is no telling when you might be faced with a triggering situation. Because of this, you must learn ways to calm yourself and your inner child if you encounter a triggering situation. Though you cannot always avoid it, you can learn to soothe your inner child and rid yourself of negative core beliefs. This chapter will guide you through various exercises to address, understand, and work through your triggers to help you and your inner child continue healing.

Before beginning, it is important to remember that you should also work through your triggers in a therapy setting with a trained mental health professional specializing in inner child work. You might want to consider practicing the less intensive inner child work exercises on your own while working through heavier exercises in the presence of your therapist. You are meant to push yourself to work through your triggers in these exercises, but if you feel that you are exerting too much energy or becoming overwhelmed, allow yourself time to recollect and practice your breathing and grounding techniques.

The Teddy Bear Therapy Exercise

Your inner child's triggers are deeply rooted in your psyche as a result of the treatment you received from your mother during childhood. Many of your triggers will result from specific incidents that left a mark on you as a child; however, you may also be triggered because of the general lack of nurturing you received from your mother.

Living a childhood full of neglect is traumatic itself and takes away your opportunity to live freely as a child, exploring and playing as children are meant to do. For many daughters of narcissistic mothers, plushies or children's toys were nonexistent during their childhood. Because of this, even simple practices like getting yourself a stuffed teddy bear can heal the part of your inner child that craves comfort and wants to experience what she was denied.

While getting yourself a teddy bear can be healing on its own, you can also practice teddy bear therapy to address specific triggers. This modified version of teddy bear therapy, inspired by Joan Sotkin (2002), helps you speak with your inner child to learn about how your triggers affect you or hold you back from embracing your inner child wholly.

To begin, find yourself a teddy bear. Other plushies also work for this exercise; however, teddy bears are most commonly used. You should choose whichever teddy bear speaks to you and brings you comfort. Consider the size of the bear compared to your own size and choose one that you can comfortably hold and cuddle in your arms.

Once you have found the right teddy bear, you should give it a name. You want to treat the teddy bear like a companion you can confide in without worrying about anyone else overhearing. Allow the teddy bear to be the confidante your inner child needs right now and feel how her presence comes through when she notices the teddy bear's comfort. If you feel silly doing this, remind yourself that this exercise is for you and your inner child only and that it is not something that has to be shared with others if you prefer to keep it private.

Once you have named your teddy bear, familiarize yourself with it as though you are getting to know a new companion. Take note of anything that sticks out to you, such as the color of the bear, the way its fur feels against your hand, if the stuffed toy is sitting up straight or slouches, or other small details that make you feel like you truly know the bear.

To maximize the effectiveness of this exercise, you should try to keep your bear by your side as much as possible. You might consider holding the bear's hand and carrying it around your house as you do other daily tasks. You may choose to sleep while holding the teddy bear or take it with you in a bag or backpack when you go out so that you can still feel its presence.

When you face a triggering situation, you can turn to your bear to vent and let your emotions run free. If you feel unhappy, describe how you feel to the bear. If you are anxious, explain what triggered your anxiety and how you feel. The teddy bear is there to listen to you without judgment or interruption. Try to use "I" statements when you are talking to your teddy bear, saying things such as "I feel upset," "I feel angry," "I feel betrayed," etc. In this private moment, give yourself the space to truly open up and vocalize the feelings that your inner child has hidden for years.

To illustrate a situation where you would use the teddy bear method, imagine that you are struggling at the end of a relationship with someone that was very close to you. You are naturally grieving over the loss during this time and likely feeling a plethora of emotions, many unpleasant. Instead of bottling up these emotions and allowing them to fester, turn to your teddy bear. Begin by telling your teddy bear what you feel, returning to your "I" statements. Do not only speak from your adult perspective, and allow your inner child to share her thoughts during this time.

As your inner child speaks to you, try verbalizing what she is feeling and where this trigger originates. Are you triggered by this relationship ending because it reinforces negative ideas you were taught in childhood? Did you instantly blame yourself for the relationship ending, regardless of who initiated it? Tell the teddy bear everything you feel, good or bad, logical or illogical. Below is a sample of what you might say to your teddy bear as you speak about this situation.

My relationship with my best friend for many years ended recently. I feel sad and sorrowful, and the process of mourning this relationship is taking a toll on me. At times, I feel angry at her for leaving me behind. At other times, I feel angry at myself for not doing everything I could to keep the friendship alive. This situation has triggered something inside of me that originated from my childhood. I recall how my mother told me I was unlovable and that people would leave me no matter what. I remember how I was only supposed to trust her and no one else because everyone else was disingenuous and didn't really like me. I keep wondering if she was right, even though part of me knows that it is illogical. However, I keep falling into this pattern, and over time, I have struggled to do anything other than blame myself and hate myself more.

My instinct is to hide my inner child right now because I am afraid of dealing with the pain of her trauma and understanding her triggers. Despite this, I also feel the need to share what I am feeling and hear the words as they come out of my mouth. I understand that this situation is not necessarily my fault alone, and oftentimes, relationships come to a natural end. The conclusion of this friendship does not mean that there are not many positive friendships to come. I am lovable and worthy, and people do genuinely love me for who I am. This one relationship does not define my worth, and I will not let my trauma prevent me from embracing and loving my inner child.

Once you have finished speaking with your inner child, pick up the teddy bear and clutch it close to your chest. As you cradle it in your arms, imagine that you are also cradling your inner child. Pet the teddy bear's head as if you are rubbing a soothing hand over your inner child's head, reassuring her that everything is fine and that she is worthy of love. Keep the teddy bear in your arms and carry it with you throughout the day. When you go to bed, sleep with the bear in your arms, picturing your inner child, safe and protected by your loving embrace.

Furthermore, you may also consider saying positive affirmations when you are speaking with your teddy bear. Though the bear is perfect for venting about your triggers or negative emotions, remaining kind and gentle with yourself is important. Some things you may consider saying to your bear once you have expressed your current emotions are:

- I let go of my fear of expressing my feelings.
- I am allowed to feel my feelings, accept them, and release them.
- I release the lingering feelings of pain that have held my inner child back from loving herself.
- My inner child has my permission to express herself and her emotions freely, whether or not her emotions are positive.
- I give myself permission to love myself unconditionally and care for myself.
- I release any shame or embarrassment remaining from past traumatic events.
- I release any lingering fear of expressing myself.

Keep these reaffirming statements in mind during this exercise and throughout your day. When you feel triggered and overwhelmed, return to your teddy bear and repeat these gentle, nurturing words to soothe yourself and your inner child.

Keeping a Trigger Toolbox or Trigger Notebook

In many situations, experiencing something that triggers you is unavoidable. While you may take precautions to avoid triggering situations, there are many scenarios where these precautions hold you back from healing while forcing you and your inner child into deeper isolation. Therefore, accessing objects that you find soothing is a must when working through your triggers. There are two ways that I prefer to collect the objects that bring me calm: a trigger toolbox and a trigger notebook.

While the concepts are similar, there are key differences regarding what you choose to put in your toolbox and notebook individually. While I recommend creating both a toolbox and notebook for your triggers, your notebook is valuable because it can be carried with you wherever you go. Therefore, when you experience triggers outside of the home, you can turn to your notebook to bring about awareness and peace of mind. There is no right or wrong way to create these objects, so be sure that you are not restricting yourself during the creation process.

Making Your Trigger Toolbox

To begin this exercise, find a shoebox where you can place all of your objects. Before selecting the soothing objects you want to include in the box, take the time to decorate the box however you would like. This part of the exercise is a great opportunity for your inner child to express herself freely, so don't feel self-conscious if your box looks "childish." Remember that this process is ultimately about healing your inner child and giving her the chance to express herself in a way that she was not allowed to in your childhood.

As you decorate your box, you may consider different styles or tools to dress the box up. If possible, use a piece of colored construction paper to glue to the box and cover up any distracting logos. Then, feel free to let your inner child run wild. Perhaps she wants to draw images on the box of things that comfort her or decorate the box with glitter and stickers. Consider writing your name on the box using glitter glue to give your toolbox a creative, fun, and personal spin. Remember that there are no rules for decorating your box—do whatever speaks most to your inner child and pay attention to how she reacts to specific decorations.

Once you have decorated your trigger toolbox, you can start filling it with comforting objects that bring you and your inner child peace of mind. For instance, you may choose to fill your box with trinkets or other small items that bring you joy, whether this is a piece of jewelry, a small stuffed toy, a seashell from your favorite vacation spot, or a tiny gift given to you by a close friend.

Additionally, you can include important photographs and documents in your toolbox. If you have pictures of happy moments, place them inside your toolbox. Because you are focusing on addressing triggers alongside your inner child, you may want to include childhood photos, such as pictures, at your favorite place as a child. You can include photographs of people that bring you peace of mind and that love you unconditionally–for instance, if you have a partner, children, or best friend, you might include photos of them.

Moving on from pictures, focus on important documents that can strengthen the effectiveness of your toolbox. These documents can range from certificates that you received during your childhood education, such as your diploma, grades, letters of recommendation from your favorite teacher, or a test that you passed with the highest marks. These documents help deal with imposter syndrome and remind you of your own abilities, strengths, and achievements. You can also include a letter of acceptance to your university if you have one on hand, letters from your loved ones, or birthday cards.

Once you have selected some of the documents you want to include, you can move on to collecting any pieces of writing that bring you calm. For example, I like to fill my trigger toolbox with a list of affirmations that remind me of my inner child's strength and resilience, while filling me with hope and self-compassion. If you have writings you created as a child, you can also place these in your trigger toolbox. If your box has enough room, you may choose to place your favorite book inside of it or a book that you loved in your childhood. If you cannot fit a book, consider copying your favorite passages and placing them inside of your box.

If your inner child likes expressing herself through artwork, you can include some of her drawings or paintings in your box. You can also add small objects you use for grounding through touch or smell. Anything that helps ground you, such as the feeling of a specific type of fabric or a calming candle scent, is valuable to creating an effective toolbox.

Finally, I encourage you to add one of the letters that you wrote to your inner child in your toolbox. There will be another example and template for writing a letter specifically about your inner child's triggers further along in this chapter; however, you can select any writing that brings you calm and soothes your inner child. Ensure that this letter is gentle, compassionate, and empathetic. Remind your inner child that you are always there for her and that, even when triggered, you will give her all of the nurturing love you possibly can.

Remember that this trigger toolbox is for you, your inner child, and no one else. If you live with others, you may consider placing your toolbox somewhere private to avoid worrying about anyone else accessing it if you are concerned about this. Don't hold yourself back–while you can include the above suggestions, your toolbox should ultimately contain what speaks to you and what helps you find inner calm.

Making Your Trigger Notebook

While your trigger toolbox is a valuable asset to have at home, you will probably struggle to carry it around with you. Therefore, you need to have tools that can help you overcome your triggers and find calm when you are triggered in public. This is easily done by creating a trigger notebook that will fit in your purse or bag.

Your trigger notebook might contain similar components to your toolbox but will focus on writings, drawings, and pictures that help ground you. To start creating your trigger notebook, prioritize any pieces of writing that you enjoy. This could entail journal entries or letters to your inner child, from yourself or friends. Furthermore, you should seek quotes or lyrics that make you feel happy and comfortable. If your inner child has a favorite song or book, include snippets from them in your notebook.

Pictures and magazine cutouts are also valuable items for your trigger notebook. Crafting your trigger notebook is a fun activity to share with your inner child, and you can spend time with her going through magazines and cutting out images to glue into your notebook. Creating a collage out of magazine cuttings might include reaffirming words that you see in the magazine's advertisements or pictures of people or products that bring you joy. You should also include important photographs in your notebook that were not included in your trigger toolbox. Additionally, you can draw in your notebook and create images of you and your inner child standing together to remind you both that you are not alone.

You can also include photos of places that bring you comfort and happiness, whether this is your favorite childhood hangout spot or pictures from a friend's home. Visual representations of the places that make you feel safe are essential to recollecting yourself and overcoming your inner child's triggers when you encounter them on a trip, at work, or in any other public space. You may also add photos of your inner child's favorite comfort foods or recipes for comfort foods that you can turn to later on in the day.

If you find smells most effective in grounding you, consider spraying a thick piece of paper with your favorite perfume. You can tape this into your trigger notebook and use it as a grounding tool whenever you need something to calm and soothe your inner child. Leave some empty pages in your trigger notebook in case you want to write reaffirming phrases to help you remain calm when you encounter a trigger in public.

Write a Soothing Letter to Your Inner Child

Ultimately, you are the nurturing, loving figure in your inner child's life. Because of this, your kind words speak volumes to the wounded inner child inside of you. If you have already written letters to your inner child, then you are familiar with how impactful words of love and encouragement can be in nurturing her. One of the most effective letters that you can write to your inner child focuses specifically on her triggers and speaks to her strengths and ability to overcome her triggers.

Triggers are, more often than not, a difficult subject to broach candidly. If you struggle to complete this letter, take a break to soothe your inner child and ground yourself before returning to the letter. You can use your completed toolbox or notebook if this happens while you are writing. Below is an example of a letter written to your inner child about her triggers and how you can help her through them. You can reference this letter when creating your own to ensure that you address important aspects of your inner child's triggers.

Dear Inner Child,

I am writing to offer you my unconditional support and love, especially in the face of triggers. I apologize for ignoring your triggers in the past, and I want you to know that I am committed to rectifying this in the future. I never addressed your triggers because I was afraid of the unpleasant, painful memories they would bring up. However, I now realize that doing so was causing harm to you and myself. Recently, you have revealed more to me about your triggers and given me insights into how your triggers negatively impact you. For instance, I can tell when you are triggered by something like yelling, abrasive noises, harsh criticisms, or the end of a codependent relationship.

I know that you have experienced immense pain due to these unaddressed triggers, and I would like to apologize again. By ignoring our triggers, I have inadvertently diminished your feelings and placed myself first. I promise I will not let this happen any longer, and that I will find ways to soothe and nurture you when you feel triggered.

I placed my hope in others during our life without realizing that our strength lies with us and our willingness to work together. Instead of continuing unhealthy relationship patterns originating in our childhood, I now wish to focus on you and building our relationship. When you are triggered by something in your surroundings, I will turn to the tools we have created to soothe you. By addressing these triggers, we can identify how they originated in our childhood and take actionable steps to overcome triggers, and remind ourselves that these traumatic memories are in the past.

You deserve all the love in the world, and I promise to spend every moment giving you this love. You can trust me and come to me without any fear of judgment or condemnation. Your triggers are not irrelevant, and you do not have to hide them from me for fear that I will push you away. I promise never to ignore you or delegate you to the back of my mind ever again. I love you unconditionally, and I *will be here to guide you through your triggers and help you recognize your own worth. No matter what happens or what obstacles we face, you will always have me by your side.*

Love,

Your Adult Self

Write Your Own Letter

✎

· · • • • • • • · ·

Validating your inner child when she faces triggering situations is essential for reminding her she is loved and supported. While determining your triggers and the roots of your trauma is challenging, it is one of the most rewarding things you can do during your personal healing journey. Remember that no matter what comes, your inner child will persevere if she has your unconditional love, support, and nurturing.

Chapter Ten

Internal Family Systems Exercises

S CAPEGOAT DAUGHTERS OF NARCISSISTIC mothers must address all parts of their personality and identity to heal their inner child and better understand themselves. As you navigate inner child healing, you will recognize new parts of your identity that you may have ignored in the past. Everyone contains different sub-personalities that comprise our "internal family." By addressing your sub-personalities, you can achieve true self-compassion through learning about your childhood trauma.

Internal family systems (IFS) therapy, referred to by some as ego state therapy, is a practice that can positively impact you in many ways. However, because IFS therapy involves a thorough understanding of your past trauma and how trauma has impacted your life, you will want to complete more intensive activities in the presence of a mental health professional you can trust. While you should try to complete many IFS exercises in a therapy setting, there are smaller activities that you and your inner child can work through to introduce you to your sub-personalities and process unaddressed trauma. This chapter comprises various exercises you can complete to begin healing the different parts of your identity.

Identifying Your "Manager" Part Versus Your "Firefighter" Part

The primary roles included in your internal family are the exile, the manager, and the firefighter. If you recall, the manager part of your personality helps you manage challenging situations through logical actions that will protect you in the present and in the future. Your manager self focuses on what matters and reminds you that your trauma is not your fault. When all members of your internal family system communicate with one another, your manager self becomes a massive part of your healing.

Though the firefighter self may appear similar to your manager self, key differences exist in the functions and purposes of these parts. Your firefighter self appears when your inner child is faced with a triggering situation that you want to avoid at all costs. The firefighter enables unhealthy coping mechanisms and chooses harmful methods to ignore traumatic memories. While your fire-fighter part intends to protect your inner child, the firefighter inadvertently harms you and prevents your inner child from healing through self-destructive habits.

Therefore, it is important to recognize the difference between how your manager and firefighter parts work to protect your inner child and ensure that you are not turning to harmful coping mechanisms that cause further pain. Below are some questions (Sutton, 2022) that you can answer to distinguish between your manager and firefighter parts and identify healthier ways of coping.

Imagine that you are in a situation where your inner child is triggered. What is your instant reaction or coping mechanism? Identify the bodily sensations that come with this mechanism. What sensations accompany this part of your identity?

✎

How do you feel regarding this part of you? You do not have to label this part as a manager or firefighter yet, but consider what feelings arise in you when taking a closer look at the sensations and instinctual coping mechanisms you instantly turn to.

✎

How does this part feel about you? Is it supportive and proud of you for overcoming a trigger or protecting yourself from triggers, or is it overly critical of your inner child?

✎

Reflect on this part. Can you identify if it is a manager or a firefighter? What positive or negative purpose is this part serving in your life?

Following the Six Fs of IFS Therapy

Another valuable exercise to identify your sub-personalities and distinguish them from one another is following the six Fs of IFS therapy: find, focus, flesh out, feel, befriend, and fear. Below are questions for each step of IFS therapy to help you differentiate between your sub-personalities and understand how each part manifests in your life (Anderson, n.d.).

Find

Find, focus, and flesh out are all centered around distinguishing your parts from one another. Consider the following questions and record your responses in the spaces provided.

Identify the sensations in your body coming from one of your parts. Who needs your attention right now?

Where do you notice this part coming from?

✎

Focus

Focus on this part and turn your attention towards it. How are you able to zone in on this part of your identity?

✎

Flesh Out

Can you see this part as you focus on it? How does it look? Describe it in as much detail as possible.

✎

If you do not see this part, how else can you describe it? How do you experience it, and what is that experience like?

✎

How close are you to this part?

✎

Feel

How do you feel about this part?

✎

What can you see or experience?

✎

(be)Friend

Start developing a friendly relationship with this part. How did this part get its role?

✎

Is this part effectively doing its job in your system?

✎

How old is this part?

✎

What else would you like to know about this part?

✎

Fear

What does this part want for you?

✎

What would happen if this part stopped doing its job in your system?

✎

Welcoming All Parts of Yourself

To heal your wounded inner child by identifying all parts of your family system, you must learn to welcome and accept all parts of yourself. You can improve communication and learn more about your needs by embracing and opening communication with all parts of your system. Follow the steps below to help all parts feel welcome (Sutton, 2022).

Step One

Allow yourself to sit alone in a spot where you feel comfortable reflecting. Look inwards, placing all of your attention inside yourself. State the following out loud or in your head: "I want to help anyone that needs help, but first, I need to know all of you."

Step Two

Now, say the following out loud or in your head: "If you overwhelm me, I cannot help you."

Step Three

Make the following request to your system parts, out loud or in your head: "Please be here with me instead of taking me over.

Whenever you are prepared, let me know who you are. I will write down who you are and what I should know about you."

Step Four

Below, take notes about the part you discovered, along with the thoughts, emotions, and sensations that accompany this part.

✎

Understand Your Relationship to Each Part

Once you have identified your parts, you can move on and start analyzing your relationship with each part of your system. By doing this, you can learn crucial details about each part while identifying the role and intention of this part. Consider the questions below (Sutton, 2022) and jot down your answers in your journal. Try to dig deep to attain a true understanding of your different parts.

What role does this part play in your system? How is it working to help you manage your life?

✎

How does this part interact with and relate to other people?

✎

What is the intent of this part? Is it fulfilling its intent in your life?

✎

How is this part working to protect your inner child, whether it does so through positive or negative means?

✎

What is this part trying to protect your inner child from?

✎

Is this part happy with its job in your family system, or does it want to do something else?

✎

Identifying Parts Through Drawing

If you are having trouble identifying the parts of your family system through writing alone, then turning to artistic methods to learn about these parts can help. Identifying your parts through drawing is a wonderful way to connect with your inner child in a fun, light-hearted activity that still accomplishes its purpose. Below are some steps you can take (Sutton, 2022) to draw your family system along with your inner child, allowing for a closer union between you and your parts.

1. Take a large, blank sheet of paper. Gather other resources like your favorite colored pencils, crayons, or markers.

2. Begin drawing, doing your best not to focus on neatness. You may choose to label your drawings for each part of yourself that you identify–for instance, if this part takes on a parental role, is a perfectionist, or is lighthearted and a jokester.

3. As you draw various parts of yourself, connect them to one another. Identify connections you find to be the most important, such as a connection between your inner child and your parental self. You can create a sort of web that helps you visualize how all of your parts are interconnected.

4. Add colors, shapes, or other details that indicate the parts you feel optimistic about and the parts that cause you to feel pessimis tic–i.e., identify parts that are compassionate, critical, judgmental, etc.

5. Once you have completed your picture and your web, reflect on what you and your inner child have created. In the spaces below, identify each part and describe how you feel about each sub-per-sonality: Are these parts good or bad? Neutral? Why do you think your parts are the way they are? ✎

Visualizing the Path of Self

IFS exercises may also involve visualizations and meditations that you find effective for connecting with your truest self. The "path of self" visualization exercise, as described by Sutton (2022), helps you explore the different parts of yourself while identifying a clearer route forward for inner child healing. Follow the steps below to complete this visualization and reunite with the parts of yourself that have gone missing.

1.   Begin by finding a comfortable place where you can be alone and free from distractions. Take some deep, relaxing breaths, noticing how the air flows through your body.

2.   Close your eyes and envision a path. This path can appear to you in many ways. For instance, you may picture a cobblestone path leading to a calming place or a clear path in the forest, where you are surrounded by nature.

3.   Notice the different parts of yourself waiting for you at the beginning of this path.

4.   Open conversation with your parts. Introduce yourself to each of them and see how they respond.

5.   Ask your parts to wait at the beginning of the path as you continue on your journey.

6.   Notice how they react when you ask this of them. Do they seem hesitant and nervous? Do they not want you to go without them? If they are not comfortable with you going along the path, then you can wait until another day when they feel more comfortable.

7.   If your parts are okay with you continuing, envision yourself and your inner child moving along the path.

8.   As you progress down the path, notice any sensations that indicate your parts are thinking of or watching over you. If you notice this feeling, then some of your parts have likely remained with you. Ask these parts if they are willing to stay behind and if they are comfortable with you and your inner child continuing.

9.   Remove any remaining parts slowly and gently. As you do this, feel how your body grows lighter and how you move closer to total awareness.

10.   Allow pleasant feelings to wash over you, noticing a new-found sense of clarity after meeting your parts. Let feelings of confidence shine through as you continue to walk down the path.

11. As you notice this energy, continue to welcome it into your body and soul.

12. Pause your journey and take a moment to recognize the bliss of deeply understanding each self in your body.

13. Move along the path for as long as necessary until you feel that you have gained value from your journey.

14. Return to your room, taking a few more deep, grounding breaths. Slowly open your eyes and take in your surroundings while noticing any sensations you feel or emotions you are left with.

Reflect With Your Protector Self

The final IFS exercise that you can practice on your own involves opening communication with your protector self. This may be the manager of your system, the misguided firefighter, or even your exiled inner child that works to protect your adult mind from harm.

This exercise will require you to dig deeper into memories with your covert narcissist mother. If you are uncomfortable doing this alone, then you can take this exercise to your therapist and try to go through it with his or her guidance. The exercise below, inspired by Sutton (2022) and altered to focus on your covert narcissist mother, will help you identify specific moments of trauma and understand how your mind has worked to protect you over the years.

1.   Begin in a comfortable location where you can be alone and free from distractions. Once again, take deep, steady breaths and allow your eyes to close.

2.   Imagine your mother in a room where she cannot exit. The room is surrounded by walls, one of which contains a one-way mirror. Look at her through this mirror, noticing how she acts and reminding yourself that she cannot see or hear you.

3.   Have your mother do or say things that would upset you and your wounded inner child. Take caution during this step, and remember not to overwhelm yourself as you dive into past memories.

4.   Pay attention to how your body reacts as your mother does or says things that upset you. Feel how your protector part makes herself known to you. You might notice this through physical sensations like an increased heart rate, tense muscles, short breaths, noticeable emotions, or permeating thoughts.

5. View your mother through the eyes of your protector to understand how she views what is happening. Remind your protector that she cannot see you and that you do not have to enter the room and face her–you are simply observing.

6. Speak gently to your protector self, reminding her that you are safe and hidden. You are not at risk right now and should remind your protector of this.

7. Ask your protector if she can separate her energy from your own. If your protector is ready, gently encourage her to separate from you and remove her energy from your body.

8. Once your protector has removed her energy, take note of any sensations in your body. Has your heart rate returned to its normal pace? Are your muscles more relaxed? Can you breathe deeply again?

9. Identify any thoughts or emotions you are feeling.

10. Look at your mother and notice how she appears now compared to the start of this exercise. Is she still acting out, or has she given up?

11. If you were to go inside the room and stand with your mother without your protector by your side, how would you feel and react?

12.   Ask your protector if she can trust you. If she is unable to, ask what is holding her back and how you can strengthen the trust between you.

13.   Sit with your protector for as long as necessary. When you are ready, thank her for her support during this visualization and the trust she has placed in you so far.

14.   Focus once again on your breathing, taking deep and steady breaths, and paying attention to how it feels as the air fills your body with life. Return your attention to the room you are sitting in and jot down any notes in your journal about your experience.

·· • • •· • • ··

Healing your wounded inner child means you must heal every part of yourself, even the parts you have forgotten. By expanding your mind and welcoming all positive and negative parts of you without judgment, you can continue to understand the experiences of your inner child and how your other parts have helped or unintentionally harmed her throughout the years.

Chapter Eleven

How You Can Re-parent Your Inner Child

O NE OF THE FINAL steps of individual inner child healing work is learning to effectively re-parent your wounded inner child. As you are now aware, your inner child needs the nurturing love and care that one would expect from a parental figure in her life. By offering her your unconditional love and support, you can truly heal her wounds and strengthen your relationship with one another.

This chapter will guide you through various re-parenting exercises to help your inner child achieve ultimate healing. While the term "re-parenting" will be used throughout this chapter, remember that you do not have to think of yourself as her mother per se. Because of the hatred or animosity that you feel towards your own mother, approaching these exercises from the position of a parent may be challenging, frustrating, or ineffective. If this is the case for you, you can take on the role of a mentor or teacher for your inner child.

What Does My Inner Child Need From a Parental Figure?

Before diving deep into re-parenting exercises, you must identify what your inner child requires from her parental figure and the attributes she associates with a loving, nurturing adult. Below is a checklist to help you understand what your inner child expects from these exercises and how you can fulfill her needs. While many of the positive attributes below may speak to you, try to check off the five that are most relevant to your wounded inner child. Once you have begun working on developing these attributes, you can always return to the checklist to see how else you can become the parental figure your inner child needs.

- Patient
- Generous
- Witty
- Humorous
- Understanding
- Selfless
- Forgiving

- Kind
- Sincere
- Empathetic
- Leader
- Brave
- Thoughtful
- Resilient
- Peaceful
- Cooperative
- Supportive
- Responsible
- Role model
- Respectful
- Encouraging
- Expressive
- Affectionate
- Gentle
- Positive
- Honest

Once you have identified the five attributes you want to focus on during the re-parenting process, jot down a few brief notes below to describe the emotions, intents, and actions you associate with each parental attribute.

✐

Creating a Life Pie Chart

Part of preparing yourself to re-parent your wounded inner child is identifying what is lacking in her life. Specifically, you will want to identify how your mother failed to parent you in different areas of your life. Creating a "life pie chart" will help you accomplish this goal and encourage genuine self-awareness that makes it possible to truly nurture your inner child. Follow the steps below (Kristenson, 2022) to create your own life pie chart and begin brainstorming ways to help your inner child heal.

1. Take a blank piece of paper and draw a large circle with a pencil.

2. Slice your circle into 8 parts and label the parts as follows: friendship, hobbies, work, faith, knowledge, health, and family. If any of these labels don't speak to you, feel free to create some of your own.

3. Go through each slice of your life pie and jot down some notes about how you have developed in this part of your life. If you feel that you have significantly developed, place a dot toward the circle's edge. If you feel that you have not developed or have regressed, place a dot closer to the circle's center.

4. Draw a line that connects all of your dots together.

5. Erase the outer circle of your life pie chart.

6. Take a look at the remaining dots and the lines connecting them. Notice which areas are lacking most and any spot where the chart is skewed. Try to identify why it is skewed this way and anything that may have led to this.

7. By doing this, you are encouraging self-awareness and gaining valuable insights into how your inner child's life is lacking and what must be done to improve these areas.

8. Brainstorm ways to improve the parts of your life where you are lacking.

Re-parenting Journal Prompts

As you determine your path of re-parenting your inner child, it is helpful to go through some prompts that encourage you to write about specific ways that you can help your inner child heal. Listening to what your inner child has to say, answer the prompts below in as much detail as possible in your personal journal.

What thoughts, emotions, or sensations is your inner child experiencing right now?

✎

What are some concrete ways to help your inner child in the areas of her life that are still lacking?

✎

Which area or areas of improvement identified in your pie chart is your inner child most afraid of? Do you know why she is afraid of this? If not, are you able to communicate with her to understand why?

✎

Look back at the attributes you selected on the re-parenting checklist. Why do you think these attributes spoke to your inner child? How can you implement these attributes into your actions?

✎

Imagine a scenario where you let your inner child down by accident. How can you rectify these mistakes and show your inner child that you are committed to doing better for her?

✎

Think of a time in your childhood when your mother or another parental figure disappointed you. Describe what you wish they had done in this situation. ✎

What is the most important message you hope to convey to your inner child through re-parenting?

✎

How can you make your inner child feel safe and protected?

✎

What is one thing you can do with your inner child today to start the re-parenting process?

✎

Letter to Re-parent Your Inner Child

The effectiveness of writing letters to your inner child is perhaps most prominent when writing to re-parent or take on a nurturing parental role. By writing a re-parenting letter to your wounded inner child, you can show her the love and compassion she needs while validating her experiences. This letter will not only acknowledge her experiences, but will contain actionable ways that you can nurture and care for her.

You may choose to use some of your responses to the questions above to guide you through the letter and identify what your inner child needs to hear from you. Additionally, you can follow the example below as a template to guide you through writing a re-parenting letter to your inner child. Again, remember that you do not necessarily have to write this letter as though you are your inner child's mother–any parental figure, including teachers or mentors, will do.

Dear Inner Child,

Recently, I have begun noticing your presence in my life and how you have grown throughout the years. I am beyond proud of you for your endurance during the toughest times in our life, and I appreciate how you have aimed to protect me from our shared past. However, I have not taken enough time to recognize how I have failed you over the years and how I can take action to ensure that this never happens again.

Right now, I can sense that you feel some apprehension about allowing me to fully take on the role of a parental figure in your life. I understand why you feel this way, especially because I have consistently attempted to deny our experiences, pain, and lingering trauma. Your fears are valid, and I hope that I have shown you recently that you can trust me. If you are still hesitant, I hope my continued work will show you that I want to nurture and love you as my own.

While the road ahead of us may seem bumpy, I intend to guide you through any obstacles we face and protect you at all costs. You deserve the best that the world has to offer, and I wish to give you all of my unwavering love. You are more special than you know and more powerful than you can imagine. I am endlessly inspired by you and awestruck by your resilience. Now, however, I want to take the weight of the world off of your shoulders and allow you to live as a child, free of parental responsibilities or worries.

This week, I plan to engage in numerous activities with you that I think you will find entertaining and uplifting. For instance, I would like for us to spend today creating artwork and drawing anything that brings us joy and comfort. I know that it will take time for you to completely heal, but I am dedicated to doing whatever I can to help you understand your value. I promise to keep you safe and love and nurture you every day. I support you no matter what and think you are perfect just the way you are.

Tomorrow, I would like to watch your favorite movie with you. We can snuggle up together on the couch and put on a movie that brings back the happiest moments of our childhood. I hope you will continue sharing your favorite activities with me because I want to experience all of them with you. I would love to go to the park with you this week to play and explore. Afterward, I want to take you to a bookstore to get your favorite novel that we can read together.

More than anything else in the world, I want to nurture and love you. You are beyond worthy of the wonderful things the world has in store for you. I am so grateful for all you have done for me, and I hope that I can give nurturing back to you tenfold. No matter where life takes you, know that I will be by your side, cheering you on and supporting you in every way you need. I love you endlessly.

Love,

Your Adult Self

Playing With Your Inner Child

Another part of the re-parenting process is incorporating play into your life as frequently as possible. As an adult, you may feel like your life is always moving by rapidly, leaving you with little time for anything outside of work. However, by only prioritizing work and leaving yourself no time to explore new hobbies and activities, you are inadvertently silencing your inner child.

Re-parenting involves allowing your inner child to play in ways she has not been allowed in the past. It is time to stop restricting yourself and your inner child from enjoying the joys of childhood and exploring new, fun ways to play and find inner peace.

Encouraging your inner child to play helps her trust you and understand your dedication to nurturing her. Therefore, take time out of every week to allow your inner child the freedom to play as she pleases. While you cannot avoid your work entirely, try to approach daily tasks with a lighter attitude and remind yourself to take breaks throughout the day. During these breaks, you can go for a walk with your inner child, play a game on your phone or computer that she likes, or take time to draw and color.

Additionally, you should carve time out of your schedule to dedicate at least one day a week to your inner child's playful side. There are endless possibilities for what you and your inner child can do together. Whether you choose to blow bubbles, go to the park, draw, complete an obstacle course, or play in the snow, play is crucial to healing inner child wounds. By prioritizing play, you will not only connect with your inner child but also reduce her stress levels, increase her creativity, help her solve problems, and teach her the value of healthy friendships (Diaz, 2022).

Meditation to Re-parent Your Inner Child

Healing your childhood wounds is a long but rewarding process. As you move toward completing the exercises in this book, it is important to prioritize relaxing meditation practices to remain grounded. The following meditation is aimed at re-parenting your inner child and soothing her spirits. Regularly practicing this meditation, provided by Kate Tunstall (2021), will help you stay focused on your inner child and discover ways to nurture and care for her every day.

1. Find a comfortable location where you will not be interrupted by anyone else. While I prefer to complete this meditation in a chair with my back straight but not tense, you can choose from various yoga positions if you are most comfortable that way.

2. Close your eyes and begin taking deep breaths, paying attention to any areas of discomfort in your body. Adjust as needed to allow yourself to relax fully.

3. Breathe in through your nose and exhale slowly several times. As your breath exits through your mouth, envision your mind emptying its troubling and distracting thoughts, letting them float away and get caught up in the air.

4. Once your mind is emptied of any distractions, return your breathing to its normal rhythm. Notice the heaviness of your eyes and relax the muscles on your face.

5. Relax your shoulders and arms. If your hands are balled into fists, unfurl them and let them fall naturally at your side or on your lap.

6. Open your pelvis and widen your legs slightly, noticing how your feet become heavier and melt into the floor below you.

7. Enjoy the sensations that you feel in your body, allowing warmth to wash over you as your body melts into relaxation.

8. Imagine your inner child creating an image of her in your mind.

9. Slowly build the image in your mind, allowing her to come into more detail as you notice her face, eyes, mouth, posture, and anything else about her that catches your eye.

10. Observe your inner child and her expressions. Does her expression convey happiness, sadness, or something else? What is her demeanor like? What does her body language convey to you? Are there any messages you notice when you look into her eyes or see the curve of her mouth?

11. Listen and pay attention to any sounds you hear. What are the sounds?

12. Now, shift your attention to your sense of smell. What scents can you pick up on?

13. Imagine a bubble beside your inner child. The bubble is dark, filled with frames from moments in your life that have caused you pain and suffering. Watch these moments without judgment.

14. The bubble may feel sinister and evoke dark feelings, including loneliness, fear, guilt, or rejection. These are the emotions that have weighed your inner child down for years.

15. Notice how your inner child is affected by the dark bubble and the harmful core beliefs it contains. The bubble tells your inner child that she deserves what happened to her, that she is to blame, and that she is unlovable.

16. Validate her beliefs but acknowledge that they are not based in truth and do not reflect reality.

17. Imagine that your inner child is not yourself. How would you react to her beliefs? What would you tell her? How would you show her kindness and nurture her?

18. Embrace the compassion that you are giving to this child and give it back to yourself. As you breathe in, feel how compassion flows through you.

19. Reach your arms out to the child and embrace her. Hold her without any judgment and offer her reassurance that everything will be okay.

20.   Breathe in deeply, and as you exhale, give compassion to your inner child as you gently blow the bubble away from her.

21.   Notice how she changes when you blow the bubble away.

22.   Envision a new bubble forming beside your inner child, empty and ready to be filled with new, happy memories and end-less nurturing.

23.   As you move forward, collect new memories to place inside of your inner child's bubble.

24.   Over time, notice how the bubble grows and expands, full of color and joyfulness.

25.   Pause and take a deep breath.

26.   Include some positive affirmations in the bubble to help ground your inner child in the future. Add hope to the bubble and watch as your inner child notices the changes.

27.   Watch as your inner child comes out of her shell, allowing her shoulders to open and the light to return to her eyes. Allow her to explore the playful side of her that has remained hidden.

28.   Take in the pleasant emotions of this newfound playfulness and allow yourself to fully experience everything related to child-hood innocence.

29.   Embrace your inner child again until you feel a connection and reach a state of harmony with her. Breathe in and out as you feel the calm coursing through your body.

30.   Stay in this space for as long as you would like. When you are ready, hold hands with your inner child and return to the present moment, taking in everything around you.

· · · · ● · ● · · · ·

Re-parenting your wounded inner child is one of the best steps you can take to show her your true love and dedication. By com-mitting yourself to nurture and care for your inner child, you simultaneously commit yourself to heal and a brighter future, full of playfulness and newfound joy and free of the mental shackles of repressed childhood wounds.

Epilogue

WITH TIME, PATIENCE, AND compassion, you can reconnect with your wounded inner child and navigate the healing process with her by your side. When you and your wounded inner child come together, anything is possible. Moving forward, remember to always keep your inner child by your side, protecting her at all costs and giving her the care that she desperately needs.

Always be proud of yourself and your inner child for your commitment to healing, even when the path to healing is rocky and uncertain. Things will not always be easy, but your strength radiates into your inner child and shines through every step she takes towards a brighter future. By truly dedicating yourself to her happiness, you can give and receive the nurturing love that you have always deserved.

I would like to congratulate you on your dedication to healing your inner child and the gentleness of your approach. In time, the trust between you and your inner child will flourish and thrive as you gain a deeper understanding of her wants and needs. The flawed thinking patterns, negative self-talk, and harmful core beliefs that have dominated your headspace do not have to take ownership of your life. With every exercise, you take a step closer to shedding the false notions you have of yourself and recognizing that you are a person deserving of love and worthy of everything beautiful the world has to offer you.

In my mind's eye, I can see my inner child browsing through aisles at a toy store. She is small, but the way she holds herself radiates confidence that I have not seen before, a strength that I never thought possible. She scans her eyes over the shelves, looking at the dolls in front of her as I stand patiently by her side. Her eyes light up as they land on a specific doll, donned in a royal blue dress and hair down to her waist. I see endless love in her eyes as she picks the doll up off the shelf, the same love radiating in my eyes as I watch her do so.

I look back to my inner child on the beach about a week ago, playing in the waters and laughing so hard her eyes crinkle at the corners. She is happier than I have ever seen her, and the pure joy and playfulness she carries are brighter than the sun warming her skin. Her legs are covered in warm water, and she stares at the fish she notices in the clear blue sea. She smiles without realizing it, happiness overtaking her and parting the dark clouds that have spent so long hanging over her head.

My inner child is happy, pampered, and, above all, loved unconditionally. I give her everything I have to give, and I accept her for who she is, not who others say she should be. The cold, dark forest with trees stretching to the sky, the one she has existed in for years, is no longer there. Instead, she is surrounded by warmth, by the sun, by gentle embraces, and loving words.

Stepping into the water with her, I put a comforting hand on my inner child's shoulder. She looks up at me and flashes me a brilliant smile, and I feel all the love in the world surging through my heart. She turns back to the water and splashes around, giggling and dancing and embracing the beauty of this newfound life—a life that, no matter what is to come, I will always fight to give her.

About Author

Ella is a passionate life coach, wife, and loving mother of three beautiful children. She is someone who has personally survived maternal covert narcissistic abuse, and whose healing process took many years, but was remarkably successful in the end. As a life coach, Ella guides her clients to achieve their goals and address the emotions that are holding them back in life, approaching each individual with a level of compassion and deep, genuine understanding. Drawing on her own experiences as well as her research, she writes her books to help every victim of covert narcissistic abuse put their past behind, to not substitute, but complement therapy, and to help them begin the healing process. Ella knows that no victim of narcissistic abuse is ever really alone, despite how isolating the victim's experience can feel. Ella understands that having a narcissistic parent can affect you long after you have left home, and her biggest hope is to help people realize that they do not have to live with this trauma forever. She uses her books as a way to provide readers who have suffered from maternal narcissistic abuse with the compassion, empathy, and validation that they have been longing for. No matter what you have been through, Ella knows from her own journey that you have the inner strength to achieve the life you deserve.

Find out more about Ella at www.ellalansville.com

Follow on Instagram @ellalansville

References

ANDERSON, F. G. (N.D.). 6 step IFS process to jumpstart healing. PESI Inc. Retrieved August 25, 2022, from https://www.pesi.com/blog/details/1511/6-step-ifs-process-to-jumpstart-healing

Davenport, B. (2022, June 23). 5 soothing meditation scripts for letting go and finding inner peace. Mindful Zen. Retrieved August 21, 2022, from https://mindfulzen.co/meditation-scripts-letting-go

Diaz, B. (2022, June 6). Awaken your inner child to the joys of play. Chopra. Retrieved August 25, 2022, from https://chopra.com/articles/awaken-your-inner-child-to-the-joys-of-play

Hanh, T. N. (2011, April 5). Healing the child within. Mindful.

Retrieved August 2, 2022, from https://www.mindful.org/heali
ng-the-child-within/

Harrison, P. (2014, May 13). How To Do Vipassana Meditation
Properly. The Daily Meditation. Retrieved August 21, 2022, from
https://www.thedailymeditation.com/vipassana

Harrison, P. (2015, March 1). Meditation To Control Emotions
& Raise EQ. The Daily Meditation coaching sessions. Retrieved
August 2, 2022, from https://www.thedailymeditation.com/con
trol-emotions

Hauck, C. (2018, October 11). A 10-minute meditation to work
with difficult emotions. Mindful. Retrieved August 2, 2022,
from https://www.mindful.org/a-10-minute-meditation-to-wor
k-with-difficult-emotions/

Kristenson, S. (2022, January 16). How to reparent yourself: A
7-step guide. Happier Human. Retrieved August 25, 2022, from
https://www.happierhuman.com/reparent-yourself/

Perkal, Z. (n.d.). How to find your inner child as an adult. Wan-

derlust. Retrieved August 10, 2022, from https://wanderlust.co
m/journal/find-inner-child/

Rettger, J. (2019, October 20). Let go of the past: A meditation practice. Sonima. Retrieved August 2, 2022, from https://www. sonima.com/meditation/mindful-living/let-go-of-the-past/

Sotkin, J. (2002, July 16). Teddy bear therapy. Prosperity Place. Retrieved August 21, 2022, from https://www.prosperityplace.c om/teddy-bear-therapy/

Sutton, J. (2021, July 7). Authenticity coaching toolkit: 13 Assessments, Scales, & worksheets. PositivePsychology.com. Retrieved August 10, 2022, from https://positivepsychology.com/authenti city-assessments/

Sutton, J. (2022, February 25). Internal Family Systems therapy: 8 worksheets and exercises. PositivePsychology.com. Retrieved August 25, 2022, from https://positivepsychology.com/internal-fa mily-systems-therapy

Tunstall, K. (2021, February 12). Inner child meditation: Free meditation script to connect with your inner child. Refined Prose. Retrieved August 25, 2022, from https://www.refinedprose.com /inner-child-healing-meditation/

Webb, J. (2019, July 14). A healing worksheet for childhood emotional neglect (also useful for therapists!). Psych Central. Retrieved August 2, 2022, from https://psychcentral.com/blog/childhood-neglect/2019/07/a-he aling-worksheet-for-childhood-emotional-neglect-also-useful-for -therapists#1

Webster, B. (n.d.). Inner Child Healing Exercises: Validate and Differentiate. Bethany Webster. Retrieved August 21, 2022, from https://www.bethanywebster.com/blog/inner-child-heali ng-exercises/

Winston, D. (2018, November 6). A meditation on your self-critical voice. Mindful. Retrieved August 18, 2022, from https://w ww.mindful.org/a-meditation-on-your-self-critical-voice/

Printed in Great Britain
by Amazon

27583709R00128